# SWEET TEA & SNAP PEAS

*Life changes,
but a couple things
stay the same.*

## McCAID PAUL

ALSO BY MCCAID PAUL

*Dead River*
*Mooch & Marlow*
*The Forgotten Headline*
*Secret Trust*
*Buried Truths*
*Hidden Places*

This book is a work of fiction. Names, characters, places, and incidents either are products of the author's imagination or are used fictitiously. Any resemblance to actual events, locales, or persons, living or dead, is entirely coincidental.

Copyright © 2024 McCaid Paul

All rights reserved. Printed in the United States of America. No part of this book may be used or reproduced in any manner whatsoever without permission from the author, except in the case of brief quotations embodied in critical articles or reviews.

Summary: Eleven-year-old Clint Boone, a worrisome farm boy who despises life's changes, lives with his pea-shelling, sweet tea-drinking grandparents. After they take in a hyperactive seven-year-old named Rhett, Clint struggles to come of age in the shadow of his unexpected new sibling.

Cover Illustration and book formatting by © 2024 Damonza
Edited by Josh Vogt
Author Photo by Amanda Bosenberg
eBook ISBN: 979-8-218-35894-5
Paperback ISBN: 978-1-7357299-8-5
Hardcover ISBN: 978-1-7357299-9-2

To my grandparents, for the sweet
tea and endless support,

And to Nathaniel, for mentioning the
snap peas that inspired this book

# FOREWORD

In 2022, while I was writing *Sweet Tea & Snap Peas*, I stumbled upon this quote by Charles and Ann Morse: "A child needs a grandparent, anybody's grandparent, to grow a little more securely into an unfamiliar world." This quote perfectly encapsulated the message and heart of my work in progress.

Growing up, my grandparents were my superheroes. They still are. There's a charm in their existence, in their spunk, their sense of humor, their vernacular, and their stories. Their charm has never dulled, and to this day, I have never loved them more.

*Sweet Tea & Snap Peas* is a tribute to grandparents and the South. It's funny, it's sad, it's hopeful, it's nostalgic. While the plot is fictional, this story is based on real people and real memories. Full of humor and heart, it's a little tale about life's changes, the struggles of growing older, and learning to love the people in your life while you have them.

To be honest, I wrote this story for myself; it was a way for me to cope with the loneliness of missing my grandparents while I was miles away at college. In doing so, this story brought me back to my childhood—to sitting on my grandparents' front porch, sipping sweet tea and laughing until my ribs hurt as they told the funniest stories I'd ever heard; to Friday nights on my grandparents' couch as the sounds of their playful bickering and pea pods snapping between their fingers lulled me to sleep; to chaotic church services, and early-morning talks with my grandpa about fighting in Vietnam. I'm only releasing this story out of hope that it might help others deal with lonesomeness, just as it helped me.

In writing this book, I realized that there's a youthful connection, an undeniable bond, between children and older people. And it's the older person's ability to tell a story that draws the child in; makes them feel safe and loved beyond measure.

Like Charles and Ann Morse said: "A child needs a grandparent, anybody's grandparent, to grow a little more securely into an unfamiliar world."

But a grandparent also needs a child. To live longer, to smile more, and to learn to love all over again.

*Sweet Tea & Snap Peas* is a quiet story—some might not understand it, and I'm okay with that. If anything, I hope it helps you appreciate the people in your life a little more. And I hope you find comfort in the story of Clint, Ella, Henry, Rhett, and Aunt Theresa just as I did.

# 1

## SWEET TEA & SNAP PEAS

A MIDDLE SCHOOL restroom is where pride goes to die.

I close my eyes and I'm there, standing in the musty-smelling boy's restroom. I imagine gray walls scribbled over in black Sharpie, cracked mirrors, paper towels all over the floor, and missing ceiling tiles. I imagine my bully dragging me into one of the stalls, his large, fleshy hands gripping my sides and lifting me up, up, up over the toilet. I imagine the scent of urine, and the sight of the toilet bowl clogged with paper and old food—

"Clint." Grandma's voice makes my eyes jolt open, pulling me out of my daydream. I'm back—back in my grandparents' living room with its green walls, black fireplace sitting atop a brick hearth, and shiny hardwood floor. "Is everything alright? You're mighty quiet tonight." She looks up from the bowl of shelled peas nestled on her lap, staring at me over the tops of her gold-rimmed bifocals.

"Yeah," I say, sitting up on the couch that Grandma bought on sale at Ralph's Discount Furniture Outlet.

"Yes *ma'am*," Grandpa says from the black leather recliner beside Grandma's, as he picks around in the giant, metal bowl of peas resting on his lap.

"Yes ma'am. I'm just tired."

It's not a lie, but it's not exactly the whole truth.

The past hour, while they've been watching a rerun of *America's Got Talent*, I've been thinking about school, which starts back sooner than I'd like. I'll be in sixth grade. I'm not ready, and I'm not sure I'll ever be. I've seen enough movies to know what middle school is like. I'd rather drive fenceposts, dig ditches, or plow the fields on my grandparents' farm from sunup to sundown than start sixth grade in a new school with so many unfamiliar faces, locker combinations, bullies, and dirty restrooms. Will I fit in? Will I even have friends? Will people still make fun of my southern accent?

A pod snaps between Grandma's fingers, and then a pea clinks against the side of her metal bowl. "Clint, watcha thinkin' about over there?"

I'm convinced grandmas have a sixth sense for knowing when something's wrong.

I open my mouth to speak but Grandpa interrupts me. "Ella, you're missing it," he says, staring at the TV.

"Is that a...*singing clown*?" Grandma rolls her eyes. "Henry Boone, turn off that nonsense. I've had enough of this show."

"Are you kidding?" he says with a big grin. "Isn't

this the best thing you've ever seen?" Grandpa winks at me.

"Where's the girl with the puppet?" says Grandma. "Why can't they bring her back? You know, the triloquist."

"Ventriloquist?"

"Whatever, Henry. You know what I meant."

With the bowl of peas balanced on her lap, Grandma reaches for a sweaty glass of sweet iced tea sitting on the end table beside her velvet green recliner. "Mmmm. That hits the spot," she says after several long gulps. Ice cubes clink inside as she sets the glass back down. "Sure you don't want some, Clint? There's a whole pitcher in the fridge."

"No ma'am, but thanks for asking."

I'm not a big tea drinker. My grandma, however, takes it to the next level. I wish I was lying when I say I've never seen the woman drink water before. It's either sweet tea or nothing at all.

"You know you shouldn't be drinking that," Grandpa says, shaking his head. "Doc's not gonna be happy."

"Oh, hush. What'd he tell you about those Diet Cokes you're always drinking? We're all gonna die of something. If sweet tea kills me, at least I'll go out happy."

Truthfully, I'm not sure how she hasn't developed diabetes by this point. It's no secret her tea is sweet enough to kill fruit flies.

The television is now playing a commercial for car insurance.

"What's that? An ostrich?" asks Grandma.

I shake my head. "I think it's an emu."

Grandpa scratches his scalp, the hairs on his head resembling pale-gray toothbrush bristles. "You know, Ella, it looks just like your second cousin."

"Shut your trap." I watch Grandma pinch a pea pod between her thumb and forefinger. She must notice me staring. "Clint," she says again, "are you sure you're alright?"

With a sigh, I tell her the truth: "No. Not really. I'm…worried."

"I can tell," she says. "Watcha worryin' over?"

"Middle school." I pick at a piece of fuzz on the couch. "I don't think I'm ready."

"So that's what this is about." She sighs, trailing a hand through her curly gray hair. "I won't lie to you: middle school is a big change. But trust me when I say it ain't nothing to worry over."

"Don't listen to her," Grandpa says. "She barely made it to the eighth grade."

Grandma picks up a fly swatter from the end table and playfully slaps him across the shoulder with it. "I've had about enough of your mouth," she shouts.

Grandpa laughs until his face is the same color as Grandma's rose lipstick. "Come on, Ella. You know it's true."

"It probably sounds crazy," I say, thinking aloud, "but what if I don't have any friends? What if I have no one to talk to at lunch? What if I get lost? Or what if some guy sticks my head down the toilet?"

I keep my biggest worry to myself: What if I'm mocked again for my accent? I don't want Grandma and

Grandpa to think I'm ashamed of how I talk or how I sound to other people, but deep down, I am.

It all started last school year when several of my classmates teased me because of my southern drawl. They thought I couldn't hear them, but I could.

"Look, it's Cowboy Clint. He's the only person that can make *Clint* rhyme with *plant* instead of *mint*."

"He's a little slow…just like he talks."

"Bet he eats cornbread for snack."

"All he's missing is a mullet."

"Looks like Joe Dirt's long-lost brother."

At a new school, with the same students from my fifth-grade class and new ones graduating from Mossy Bend Academy across town, I'm certain the teasing is bound to get even worse. What nicknames will they have for me this time? Huckleberry Clint? Clint Clampett? Clint the Cable Guy?

"Hon," says Grandma, "you're going to worry yourself sick. Lord only knows how you don't have an ulcer."

She's right; I take worrying to the extreme. She's always teasing me about it, even though she knows that I have good reason to be a worrywart.

I look above the fireplace, my gaze fixing on a picture frame resting on the mantel. My parents smile back at me—Mom with her soft, kind eyes, and wavy chestnut-colored hair. Dad, with his crooked grin, crew cut hair, and large brown eyes.

Staring at my parents' photo makes me remember the day I wish I could forget.

I remember Mom and Dad dropping me off just

down the road at Grandma and Grandpa's house so that I could spend the weekend with them.

I remember the shrill ring of the doorbell later, and Grandma going to answer it.

I remember following her to the door and noticing the two cops standing on the porch.

I remember Grandma asking, "How can I help you?" and the cops shuffling their feet before one of them said, "Do you know Laurie and Hunter Boone?"

"Yes? Is everything alright?" Grandma asked.

Most of all, I remember the silence, the heavy, horrible silence. Grandma, covering her mouth with a trembling hand. Her eyes widening.

"There was an accident," the other cop said, so soft I could hardly hear her. "I'm so sorry, ma'am."

"Are they okay?" I asked, failing to understand.

I remember Grandma turning and wrapping me up, her arms the answer: Mom and Dad were gone.

Since that day five years ago, change has been my nemesis. Change replaced my hope with dread. Change took my parents and left me behind. I hate the thought of change.

I glance away from the picture, staring down at my chewed fingernails, gnawed to the quick, the skin around them raw.

"Middle school can be exciting. In fact, I had my first kiss on my first day of sixth grade," Grandma says.

"And we haven't heard the end of it since." Grandpa rolls his eyes. "You know, you never told me the feller's name."

"Well, Henry, it was a long time ago."

"Right. That's what old people say when they can't remember straight."

Grandma ignores him and looks at me. "You'll be fine, Clint. Just give it a few days. You'll adjust."

I look down at my lap. "I wish things didn't have to change."

"Change is inevitable," Grandma says, "like turning gray or going bald."

"Doesn't mean I have to like it," I mumble, picking at a hangnail.

"Change is a part of life, son," says Grandpa. "But you want to know two things that never change?"

"Death and taxes?" Grandma asks.

"No," Grandpa says. "Sweet tea and snap peas."

Grandma smiles and nods her head. "That's right."

The television is now playing an underwear commercial.

"Goodness gracious. She could at least put on some pants," Grandma says.

"There ain't any secrets there," adds Grandpa.

"In my day, people did not dress like that."

"Good. 'Cause if they looked anything like your kinfolks, I'd poke my eyes out."

With a sigh, I lean back on the couch and close my eyes, falling asleep to the soothing sound of their playful bickering and pea pods snapping between their fingers.

# 2
# GRANDPA'S BOOTS

AT SIX A.M. the next morning, I'm sitting on the front porch swing when Grandpa comes out to feed the chickens and cows. The sweet smell of pollen lingers in the humid air, the farm calm and still, quiet except for the chirp of birds, the occasional crow of a rooster, and the slight squeak of the windmill. In a few hours, the Florida heat will be almost unbearable, and the summer sun will pound down on the farm. The air will pulse with cicadas and fill with the bleating of goats, the buzzing of carpenter bees, and the metallic trill of hummingbird wings.

Sandy, our rusty-red cocker spaniel, sits at my feet, staring up at me. When the front door opens with a gentle creak, she pays it no mind. She just keeps staring, as if she can tell something is wrong.

A second later, Grandpa steps onto the porch, the

door slipping shut behind him as he whistles Hank Williams' "Hey, Good Lookin'." Chest hair pokes out between unbuttoned holes in his navy-blue work shirt, which I have no doubt will be dripping with sweat before the morning is over. Whenever he peels off that sweat-drenched shirt before lunch and turns his back to me, I can always spot the round, nickel-sized scar on his lower back—a permanent mark from the Vietnam War.

"Well, someone's up early," he says, bending down to pick up a pair of muddy, well-worn, brown work boots sitting beside the front door.

"Couldn't sleep," I tell him.

"Still worried about school?"

"I'm always worried about school."

Sandy hardly moves an inch as Grandpa steps over her and sits beside me with a big sigh, the swing creaking under his weight. He smells like Old Spice aftershave and laundry detergent.

"Hmmm," he says, cramming his foot into a boot. "Well, let me tell you a story."

"About middle school?"

"No, about 'Nam."

Sandy thumps her tail against the ground, looking at Grandpa like she's listening too.

"When I turned eighteen, I got the biggest shock of my life." He props his foot on the edge of the swing and begins to lace the boot's grimy brown strings.

"What was it?" I ask.

"Well, it was a draft notice for me to join the Army."

"Oh."

"I didn't like it much. In fact, I didn't want to go.

Mama didn't want me to go either, 'cause she knew if I did, chances were I wouldn't come back."

*I guess middle school is nothing compared to being drafted*, I think.

"I worried over it something awful," says Grandpa. "I thought: who's going to help Mama when I'm gone? Who's going to plow the fields or split the firewood or help your crazy Aunt Theresa every time she gets her car stuck in a ditch?"

Sandy's ears twitch and she yawns.

"But I found that worrying didn't make things any better," Grandpa says. "In fact, it didn't change a thing."

"Well, how do I make the worries go away?"

"You get through it," he says, "like we all do. Like I did. You keep your chin up, you lace your boots up, and you keep on keeping on."

He crams his other foot in the second boot. Sometimes, on mornings like this, when I watch Grandpa put on his work boots, I imagine myself tromping through a foul-smelling Vietnam mud field in those shoes, even though, deep down, I know those particular boots haven't ever left the state of Florida. I imagine they were the same type of boots that he sprinted down a mountain slope in after being shot in the back by the Viet Cong. The same boots that he wore on the helicopter ride to the hospital ship that saved his life.

Grandpa's voice brings me back to the present. "You see, Clint...change is a part of life. I could've died in 'Nam, but I didn't. I could've stayed behind, but what would've become of me? I can bet that if it wasn't for change, I wouldn't be sitting here with you right now.

"So believe me...you'll get through this. In fact, I believe sixth grade will be your best year yet."

"Let's hope so," I mumble, even though I don't have much hope for sixth grade at all.

Several of my fifth-grade classmates squashed my hopes flat when they mocked my accent, sometimes even to my face. "Look, it's Cowboy Clint. Ain't got a brain in his noggin'," they'd say, snorting with laughter. To them, my accent made me sound dumb, even though Grandma told me not to give them the time of day. She said my accent made me unique and friendly-sounding, and that my classmates were just being ignorant. I wish I could believe her.

Still, I can't help but wonder: If I struggled to fit in at elementary school, how am I supposed to fit in at middle school, where I'm certain the eighth graders will tower over the sixth graders like giants, and bullies will circle the halls like sharks, waiting for their chance to attack Cowboy Clint.

Shaking away the thought, I bend down and give Sandy a pat on the head. She licks my fingers as if to tell me thank you.

"One of these mornings," Grandpa says, setting both feet on the ground and looking off the porch, toward the footbridge that leads across the creek at the edge of the woods, "I'll have to tell you the rest of the story."

"Okay," I tell him. "I'd like that."

He shakes his head. "It's not a happy story, but then again, life isn't always happy."

Sandy wags her tail back and forth as Grandpa stands from the porch swing, both of his knees popping.

"Getting older ain't all it's cracked up to be, is it, girl?" He scratches the spot behind Sandy's ears. To me, he looks sort of sad now after he's told his story. Sad and old.

It makes me wonder what else he's not telling me about what happened in Vietnam.

Grandpa claps his hands together. "Alright, now go on inside and wake up your grandma. Tell her I'm fixin' to starve to death."

"Yes sir."

"And if that don't work, tell her the goats are in her garden. That ought to do it."

As I go to wake up Grandma, Grandpa's words linger in my mind. *Change is a part of life. You'll get through this. I believe sixth grade will be your best year yet.*

Grandpa's right to say that change is natural, and that I will somehow survive middle school. But I'm not convinced that sixth grade will be my best year yet. Grandpa's right about most things, but I'm not so sure about this.

Deep down, I have a feeling that sixth grade *will* change everything, just not for the better.

# 3

## AALIYAH & CLINT EASTWOOD

A FEW DAYS later, with my lunch box clutched in hand and my backpack's tight, narrow straps digging into my shoulders, I'm standing beside the road with Grandma and Grandpa, waiting for the bus. I hear it before I see it, rumbling around the bend and screeching to a stop. It's still not as loud as my heart pounding in my ears.

"You've got this, Clint," says Grandpa, squeezing my shoulder.

"It'll only be a few hours," Grandma says, kissing me on the cheek. "By the time I get through with my *Golden Girls* marathon, you'll already be home."

I hug them both, tell them a quick goodbye, and trudge toward the bus, blowing out several short breaths. As I approach, the doors swing open with a hiss. Heart racing, stomach churning, I force myself up the bus steps, entering a different world.

I take the closest empty seat I can find, three rows back from the front. Soon, I'm rumbling along in the loud, cramped bus stifling with heat and sweaty, stale air. Grandma and Grandpa wave to me from the driveway beside our black iron gate, which they claim keeps the animals from running out into the road, even if secretly I know it's more to keep our nosy next-door neighbor, Ms. Jean, out of our business.

Face pressed against the glass, I watch as Grandma and Grandpa grow smaller and smaller, until the bus rounds the curve, and they're gone. After that, I slump back against the grimy vinyl seat, trying not to cry.

Eventually, the heat and smell become so suffocating that all I can think about is getting some fresh air. I try to slide down the window, but it won't budge. Great, it's jammed shut.

Even worse, when I reach down to retrieve a book from my backpack, the bus speeds over what must be a giant pothole, and my head nearly smacks the seat in front of me. With every sudden bounce and rattle of the bus, the nylon belt digs into my skin, tightening like a boa constrictor around my waist.

If this is any indication of how the rest of my day will go, then I'm doomed.

"Hey."

The peppy voice makes me jump.

A girl with brown skin and curly black hair stares down at me from the center aisle.

"Hey," she says again. "Can I sit here?"

I nod. "Sure. I don't mind."

She plops down beside me, settling her backpack on her lap. "Sorry to bother you," she says, "but those boys back there were being too loud. I couldn't even hear myself think."

"You're not bothering me," I say.

I wonder how my accent sounds to her. Does she think I sound dumb too? I wouldn't be surprised if she traded seats with someone just to get away from Cowboy Clint.

Instead, she smiles at me. "My name's Aaliyah. You know, like the singer."

"Aaliyah?"

"Yeah. R&B legend, Aaliyah. Ever heard of *One in a Million* or *Back and Forth*?"

I shake my head. "Doesn't ring a bell."

Aaliyah's eyes widen. "You're telling me that you've never heard of…forget it."

"My name's Clint. Like Clint Eastwood."

"Clint Eastwood?" says Aaliyah. "Never heard of him."

"You can't be serious. He's one of the most famous actors of all time! Maybe you've heard of *Dirty Harry*?"

"Nope." Aaliyah yawns.

"Okay. How about *The Good, the Bad and the Ugly*?"

Aaliyah shrugs.

"Unbelievable," I mumble.

The bus bounces again, making me wince. Aaliyah doesn't seem to mind.

"So, which bus stop were you?" she asks.

"Huh?"

"Which stop? Like, which house?"

"Oh. It was a farm. That's where I live."

Aaliyah puts a finger to her chin, sort of like Grandpa when he's mulling over things. "Hmmm. I think I'd remember that. Is it a big farm?"

"Sort of. We've got a dozen chickens, ten cows, a donkey, and some goats. We've even got a windmill."

"Cool. What else do I need to know about you, Clint? Got any siblings? I've got six."

"Six? That sounds awful. I'm the only child."

"Lucky," Aaliyah says, crossing her arms over her chest.

"But I live with my grandparents. How about you?"

"What? No fair! I wish I lived with my grandparents. I bet they let you watch whatever, whenever you want."

"Well, not exactly—"

"My granny does. We mostly just watch movies and eat popcorn. And she lets me stay up as late as I want. It's the best!"

"My grandparents mostly fuss, drink sweet tea, and shell peas. They like to tell stories, too. They tell the best stories when they're shelling peas."

"Peas? What kind of peas?"

"Mostly purple-knuckle hulls with snaps. They love snaps."

"What are snaps?"

"They're the ones that are too small to shell. They look like little green beans. Typically, no one wants them since they're hard to shell and they don't look like much. But my grandparents mix them in with the rest of the peas. They don't like wasting anything, so they just use them instead of throwing them away."

We talk and talk until I learn a few more things about Aaliyah: she's in the seventh grade, her favorite color is fuchsia pink, and she hates cafeteria food. I don't know what's more surprising: the fact that she never mentions my accent, or the fact that she already treats me like a friend.

Before long, the bus crawls and rumbles to a stop outside the red brick walls of Mossy Bend Middle School. The bus doors flap open, and soon students are running, pushing, and stomping down the narrow aisle to be the first ones off.

Aaliyah rolls her eyes. "Geez, can't they wait their turn? We're all going to the same place. Last time I checked, there isn't anything special about getting to school any earlier than we have to."

Aaliyah's comment reminds me of something Grandma says whenever I ask why she never shows up on time for doctor appointments. *There's no advantage to being early, son,* she always tells me. *You've still got to wait. Besides, the last time I showed up early, I waited around until I got the bladder spasms.*

Aaliyah and I are going to get along just fine.

When we both stand from our seats, Aaliyah turns to me and says, "Remind me to bring my earbuds and let you listen to Aaliyah sometime."

"Okay. But only if you watch a movie with Clint Eastwood."

Aaliyah frowns. "Who?"

She must notice the puzzled look on my face because

she tosses her head back and laughs, spontaneous and shrill, sort of like Grandma when she realizes her misplaced glasses have been on top of her head the entire time or when she's had a bit too much cold medicine. It's so infectious that I start to laugh too.

"Okay, Clint," she says, stepping into the center aisle. "Sounds like a deal."

I sling my backpack strap over my shoulder. "See you this afternoon?"

"Of course," she says, smiling back at me. "And good luck on your first day of middle school. You're going to be just fine."

"I think so too," I say, but I don't believe it.

# 4

## JESUS & BARTHOLOMEW

MIDDLE SCHOOL IS nothing like I expected. For one, there are no lockers. It's also smaller than I thought it would be, and according to our principal, Mrs. Mitchell, during our grade-level talk in the auditorium, there are only one hundred and fifty students in my sixth-grade class.

The bell doesn't sound anything like the ones in the movies, either. This one is deeper and less obnoxious, even if it does drone on a tad too long.

I only get lost once (okay, maybe twice). Still, I'm not late to any of my classes.

All of my teachers are nice, but old. One of them calls everyone "partner," and another wears a sweater covered in cat hair. (Ironically, her name is Catherine Hare.)

Lunch is fine, but loud. I sit with several people from

my homeroom, and they seem friendly, even if they chat about video games the entire time. I pretend to understand what they're talking about, even though one of Grandma's house rules is no video games allowed.

The worst part of the day is probably all of the cussing and shoving in the halls by the older kids. Well, and this one kid named Bart Kingsley. He sits in the row of desks behind me during seventh period.

At lunch, Bart flicked English peas off his tray at me and several others until he grew disinterested. None of us paid him much attention, which I think bored him; by not paying the guy any mind, I assumed he'd find someone else to flick peas at.

Grandpa would say that's just some people's way of saying hello. But Bart seemed like trouble, and I wanted to keep my distance. After all, I didn't want my head dunked down a toilet, especially *not* on my first day of middle school.

Now, during math, the last period of the day, Bart kicks the back of my chair. Hard.

I ignore him.

"Hey," he says, "I'm trying to talk to you."

I keep staring straight ahead and don't answer.

Our teacher, Mrs. Flynn, doesn't seem to notice; she's too busy reading and pronouncing our names from the class roster. "Velocity? Or is it Velicity?"

"Felicity," a girl in the second row says.

"Thank you, dear. How about Jesus?" Ms. Flynn scratches the tip of her nose, which is as pointy as a bird's beak. "Jesus, are you here?"

"No, no," someone says from behind me. "Not Jesus. It's pronounced hay-SOOS."

"Oh, dear. Forgive me," Ms. Flynn says, placing a veiny, wrinkled hand over her heart. "It did sound a bit majestic for a young boy."

I bite my lip to keep from chuckling.

"Clint?" she calls out next. "Clint Boone?"

I hold my hand up in the air. "Here."

"Clint? Where's Clint?"

"Right here, ma'am," I say, holding my hand a little higher.

Ms. Flynn points the end of her pencil around the room, squinting her beady eyes until she finally notices me. "Oh, there you are! Glad to have you with us, Clint."

"*Hey*. Clint." Bart kicks the back of my chair again.

"Spencer?" Ms. Flynn shrills.

Bart takes his foot off the back of my seat.

"Yeah, that's me," a guy along the front row mumbles.

"I sure do like that name," Ms. Flynn says. "*Spencer*. I used to have a dog named Spencer. He loved to chase bicycles. Bicycles, and the mailman. Do you chase the mailman, Spencer?"

I try not to laugh, but a small sound escapes my lips.

"Hey." Bart kicks the back of my chair for the third time. "What's so funny, Clint?" he whispers.

I look at Ms. Flynn, who is too busy peering down at the class roster to notice me turn around in my seat and tell him, "Nothing."

"Good," Bart says. "'Cause I wouldn't be laughing with a name like Clint. Seriously, did your great-grandma name you or something? Was she, like, married to a cowboy?"

I stare into his large eyes, then down at his large sneakered foot, still planted on the back of my chair. It smells like vinegar and moldy cheese. "Can you please move your shoe?"

"I don't know, Cowgirl. Can I?"

He's wearing a black North Face T-shirt, Nike tennis shoes, and blue jeans ripped below the knee. His face is a little too puffy, his eyes set a little too far apart, and his nose a little too piggish. Every time he speaks, a bit of spittle flies from his lips. Some of it even lands on my desk.

Once again, I turn back around and ignore him. I can only hope that he'll soon grow bored of me and pester someone else.

"Bartholomew?" Ms. Flynn trills.

"It's Bart, ma'am," Bart huffs behind me.

She sighs. "I used to go steady with a Bartholomew."

"Bartholomew?" I mumble. "Who names their kid Bartholomew?"

"Hey, Cowgirl," Bart says again. "Got something to say?"

*That's it,* I think.

I turn around and face him. "What's your problem? I don't even know you."

"You don't have to know me for me to have a problem with you," Bart says.

"What does that even mean?"

"Huh?"

"You don't make sense."

"Oh yeah? About as much sense as your dimwitted accent. And that oversized shirt you're wearing. And those Jesus sandals. And that awful military haircut. Is your dad a little soldier boy or something?"

My cheeks burn. "Don't talk about my dad."

"Why? What are you going to do about it?"

I stare at him for a moment, stare right into those large eyes of his. I could give it right back to him, but I don't want my head dunked down a toilet. I don't want to have to tell him that my dad *was* a soldier, and that war didn't kill him, but driving along the interstate did, just like it killed my mom. I don't want to have to tell him that these clothes are hand-me-downs from my grandparents, and that they took me in when I had nowhere else to go.

I don't want to tell him all that because he doesn't deserve to know. Besides, it's only the first day of school.

# 5

# THE BOY WITH THE COWBOY HAT

When the final bell rings, I snatch up my binder and backpack and rush to get out the door before Bart can follow. But all the way down the crowded hall, Bart lingers close by, weaving in and out of the other students, trying to catch up.

Sweat forms on my brow. My heart races and my steps quicken, sandals slapping the shiny linoleum floor. But no matter my pace, Bart won't seem to go away.

Once I manage to squeeze out the door for the long row of yellow buses, I look back, and puffy-faced Bart is right behind, those large eyes of his trained right on me. And when I board the bus, hurrying for my window seat just a few rows back from the front, Bart is practically on my heels.

"Get out of my way," Bart huffs, elbowing past me in the center aisle.

I watch as he stomps and shoves his way to the back of the bus.

I must stare for a moment too long, because soon I hear the sighs, groans, and disapproving tongue-clicks from those standing behind me.

"Move, moron," one of them says.

"Step on the back of those sandals, and then he'll move," someone else replies.

"Clint, I'm right here," a voice at my side pipes up.

I look down. It's Aaliyah.

"I'm so glad it's you," I say, taking a seat beside her. "How was your first day? Not too bad, I hope."

"It was...okay."

"Just okay?"

I start to mention Bart, but I bite the words back. Instead, I just nod.

"See? I knew you'd be fine. There's really not much to it."

"No, guess not," I say.

But I have a feeling there's much more to Bart Kingsley, and something tells me I've only experienced a fraction of his torture.

After I tell Aaliyah goodbye and the bus drops me off at my house, I notice three things amiss. One is the front gate, which my grandparents always keep shut but somehow must've forgotten to close today. Another is

Ms. Jean, who stares at me from across the road on her front porch, both hands on her wide hips, and a checkered apron tied around her waist. I don't have any trouble believing she stopped cooking long enough to poke her nose somewhere it doesn't belong. Right about now I bet she's wondering, just like me, why my grandparents left the gate open.

I make sure to shut it before I begin the short walk down our gravel drive.

*Do we have company?* I think to myself.

"Clint!" Ms. Jean shouts to me from across the way, but I pretend not to hear her. Grandma says Ms. Jean is as nosy as a housefly on a dinner plate, and I know not to pay our neighbor any mind.

The third and final sign that something's amiss is the boy sitting on the front porch steps between my grandparents. He's short and wiry-thin, with skin the color of caramel from the sun. He's wearing an oversized, tan cowboy hat which slips down below his ears, a wrinkled white T-shirt, baggy blue jeans, and pointy brown boots. He looks to be around seven or eight years old.

As abnormal as this day has been so far, nothing is as odd as the sight of my grandma's hand on the small boy's shoulder, or the wide grin plastered on my grandpa's face, like they've both known this child for a long time.

Even worse is that neither of them seem to notice me until I'm standing a few feet away.

"What's going on?" I ask. At the same time, I share a glance with the boy in the cowboy hat. Beneath the brim, two beady brown eyes stare back at me.

"Clint," Grandma says, dropping her hand from the boy's shoulder, "this is Rhett. He's going to be staying with us for a little while."

It takes several seconds to process her words. When I do, my belly flutters and my skin tingles. "What do you mean?"

Grandma gives me a look. The *we'll talk about this later* look.

"Rhett," Grandpa says. "How about you go on inside and get washed up for supper? We'll be there in a minute."

The boy nods, looks at me again for a second, and then stands. "Yes sir," he says softly.

The second the door closes behind him, Grandma speaks. "There's something we've been meaning to tell you."

"Who is he, and why is he here?" I blurt.

"Hold on now. I'm getting to that—"

But Grandpa cuts her off. "Here's the short version: his parents got into some trouble, and the boy needed a place to stay. He came sooner than we would've liked."

My heart races. "How long will he be here?"

Grandpa glances over at Grandma before saying, "We don't know. It might be a short while. It might be a long while. But we know you'll be good to him. Now you'll have some company besides us old folks."

I shake my head. I must not have made myself clear enough, so I try again. "Who is he?" I repeat. "Why are his parents in trouble?"

"He's a distant cousin of mine," Grandma says. "And, well, his parents got into a dispute with the law, and Rhett can't live with them right now. Look, he had nowhere else to go."

"He could've gone to live with Aunt Theresa. Besides, a little heads-up would've been nice."

"Sorry, Clint. Your great aunt hasn't had a kid in her house in twenty years. And the State people don't give you a lot of notice with stuff like this."

I ball my fists and cross my arms. "Fine. But he's not sleeping in my bed."

"We'll cross that bridge when we get to it," Grandpa says.

Grandma starts rubbing my back, but it doesn't make me feel any better. "This is going to be a big change for all of us," she tells me. "But think of it like this: Rhett is sort of like a snap pea. He might be tiny, but someone's got to give him a fightin' chance."

# 6

## RHETT, THE LITTLE RASCAL

It's only been an hour, but I'm already sick of Rhett. At dinner, he sat in my seat and drank out of my blue plastic cup. The worst part was that Grandma gave him my fork, the one with the rabbit stamped into the handle. Throughout the meal, I didn't say one word, and barely chewed my food. I was too upset to eat, let alone pretend to enjoy my roast beef and mashed potatoes.

After dinner, we sit in the living room. All the while I stare at the wall and make a mental list of all the things I already don't like about Rhett.

Number one is that he smiles at everything. Let's face it: no one is *that* happy.

Number two is that oversized cowboy hat, which Grandma can't stop touching and clearly thinks is so cute and adorable, when it is most definitely not.

Number three is that he can't keep still. He's constantly tapping his foot, his fork, or picking at the tablecloth with his Oreo-dirt fingernails.

Number four is that he hasn't spoken one word to me. How are we supposed to get along when he won't even acknowledge my presence?

Number five is that he sits in Grandma's recliner, and she lets him.

Number six is that he's even here in the first place.

"Clint." Grandma's voice interrupts me from my mental list. "How about you go on over there to the wooden box under the TV cabinet and pick us out a board game."

I stare at her for a moment, propped back in her recliner with an arm draped over Rhett's shoulder. "A board game? Why?"

"Clint, don't argue with your grandmother," says Grandpa from his recliner. Lowering his voice a little, he adds, "Sorry, Rhett. He's not usually like this."

*I can still hear you,* I think.

With a sigh, I trudge over to the wooden box beneath the TV cabinet, which is spilling over with games of all kinds. Board games and card games I've played with Grandma and Grandpa countless times over the years: Checkers, Connect Four, Candyland, Operation, Sorry!, Battleship, Uno, and my least favorite, Monopoly.

That game takes *forever*.

I read off each name aloud, purposely saving Monopoly for last.

When I'm done, Grandma says, "Alright, Rhett. Which one?"

"Hmmm." Rhett puts a finger to his chin. "How about...Monopoly!"

*Of course*, I think, rolling my eyes.

"Monopoly it is," Grandma says with a little chuckle. "That's Clint's favorite, you know." She winks at me and smiles. I don't smile back.

When I look at Rhett, the little rascal does the worst thing possible: he grins, all big and proud, showing off most of his teeth, like he knows he's doing a fine job of ruining my life.

Honestly, I don't know how much more of him I can stand. I can already tell he's going to get everything he wants, which is also going on my list of things I don't like about him. Including that stupid smile.

"Y'all go ahead," I say, handing the board game to Grandma. "I'm going to my room."

"Now, Clint," Grandpa says. "What's gotten into you? Where's that competitive spirit?"

"I'm just tired."

"When have you ever been too tired to play a board game?" Grandma asks, turning the box over to read the instructions, even though we've played Monopoly a hundred times.

"Y'all have fun." I turn on my heel and head for the stairs.

"Clint, wait. Don't act like this…"

"Come on, son. We've got company…"

Their voices trail away as I hurry up the staircase. At the top, I pause long enough to swipe a stray tear from my cheek. "My first day of middle school was fine by the way," I mumble to myself. "Just in case you were wondering."

# 7

# BOARD GAMES & BUBBLEGUM

I'M NOT SURE how long I lay in bed, staring up at the top bunk and listening to the voices and occasional laughter coming from downstairs. The sounds make my stomach tighten, my teeth clench, and my throat burn.

"Why does life have to be so unpredictable?" I grumble. "Why can't anything stay the same?" I turn onto my side and face the window, watching the sunlight fade away outside like my hope. "Why does *he* have to stay here? Why can't he go somewhere else?"

Before long, I sit up, scoot to the edge of the mattress, and shift my focus to the cherry-wood dresser beside my bed. Opening one of the drawers, I reach inside with both hands, removing a navy-blue photo album—the perfect distraction from Rhett.

As I flip through the album, filled mostly of photographs of my parents, a hard lump forms in my throat. There's one of my mother, mid-laugh, holding up a Def Leppard vinyl record, her wavy chestnut-brown hair spilling over her shoulders, pink pig slippers on her feet. She looks so young, in her early twenties, probably. There's one of my father smiling wide, wearing the same pig slippers, arms extended to the side, the flash of the camera reflected in his large brown eyes. I wouldn't be surprised if Mom took the picture as he danced a jig in our living room. There's another of him holding our old dog named Rowdy-Blue, a Blue Heeler who died when I was three. There's one of my parents, leaning in for a kiss, while Rowdy-Blue jumps in between them, his pink, drooling tongue inches from Mom's face.

It's strange seeing my parents when they were young. Seeing the clothes they once wore and the way they once styled their hair. It's like I'm intruding on private moments of their lives—a time before I existed, when I was merely a thought in my parents' minds. It's strange to think they existed before me, and it's even stranger to realize that I'm able to exist now without them. It's just not fair.

I turn the page, but the rest of the album is empty—just plastic sheaths with nothing inside them. Blank slots where photos should be stored. Blanks slots of memories never made.

I close the album and place it back in its drawer, my knuckles grazing against the side of a yellow birthday card with red and blue balloons on the cover. The front reads: *For a Special Son.*

I lift the card out into the light.

When I open it, I hear my mother's voice—it's one of those cards that lets you record yourself speak. "Happy sixth birthday!" she says. "We love you!"

"Not as much as cake," Dad adds. "But pretty close."

I chuckle, even though my throat tightens.

I close the card; open it again.

"Happy sixth birthday! We love you!"

"Not as much as cake," Dad repeats. "But pretty close."

I close it; open it for a third time. I could listen to their voices all day, and they wouldn't get old.

I don't know what I'll do when the battery eventually wears out.

"Clint?" Grandma's voice sounds from the bottom of the stairs.

I quickly put the card back, close the drawer, and lay on my side, facing the wall like I was several minutes ago. Maybe Grandma will think I'm asleep.

Her footsteps creak up the stairs, coming to a stop in my doorway.

"Clint, get up and quit that moping."

I keep still.

"Don't make me come over there."

I roll back onto my other side and face her.

"I'm not moping."

"Yes, you are. Now get up and come downstairs. We've got company, and you're not setting a good example."

"I don't feel like it," I groan.

"Seriously?" Grandma crosses her arms and cocks her head. "You're this jealous over a seven-year-old?

One who, in case I have to remind you, didn't have anywhere else to go until a couple hours ago. Put yourself in his boots for a minute. How would you feel if no one wanted you?"

"Bad."

"Exactly. And how would you feel if the only other young'un in the house made it plain and clear he didn't want you there?"

"Okay, I see your point."

She steps into the room and sits on the edge of my bed. I rise to a sitting position.

"I love you," she says, placing a wrinkled hand on my leg. "I know this is difficult for you since it's always been the three of us, but you'll be okay. You will learn to like Rhett, just as he will learn to like you. First you've got to try to get along, or it ain't going to get any better."

I swallow back the lump in my throat and take a deep breath. "I know. And I'm sorry."

"Good." She reaches forward and wraps her arms around me. She smells like baby powder and vanilla. "Now, let's go on down there and play a board game. Whadda'ya say?"

"Yes ma'am," I sniffle, wiping my nose with the back of my hand.

"Oh, and one more thing. How do you feel about Rhett sleeping in here tonight? He can take the top bunk if that's alright."

"What? You can't be serious."

She kisses my forehead, her lips making a wet, smacking sound. "See? I knew you wouldn't mind."

It's clear Grandpa lost interest in Monopoly five turns ago. He hasn't passed go except for one time all night. In fact, his pile of money is nearly depleted, but he doesn't seem to care.

"Somebody go ahead and get these last five dollars," Grandpa says in between sips from a Mason jar of sweet tea. "It's past my bedtime. You boys are killing me."

"Hey, can I have some?" Rhett points to Grandpa's tea glass.

"Sorry, son," Grandma says, sorting out her stack of money into different colored piles. "But we don't want you wetting the bed."

"What? I've never wet the bed!"

Grandpa gives Rhett a sideways look.

"Okay, maybe a few times," Rhett says, hanging his head.

"No sweet tea, and 'specially no watermelon." Grandma winks at me. "Clint should know all about that."

"Alright, Grandma," I say, my cheeks burning. "Can we get back to the game?"

But Grandma can't leave it alone. "One night, after Clint ate a pile of watermelon before bed, we heard a noise in his room. We went in there, turned on the light, and where was he? Fast asleep, peeing in the corner. Sounded like a dern' water hose."

Rhett's beady eyes pinch together as he leans back in his chair, laughing so hard his caramel-colored cheeks turn bright red and veins pop out on the side of his head.

"Oh, you're one to talk. Let's not forget about that stunt you pulled several years ago," says Grandpa.

"Who? Me?" Grandma points to herself. "You're making it up now."

"Me? Never." Grandpa turns his attention across the table to Rhett. "Some people wet the bed, some people sleepwalk, but not Ella. She sleep eats. I can't tell you how many times I've found her in the pantry with this glazed look across her face, sort of like a bear that just woke up from hibernation."

"Hush your mouth," Grandma says, holding up her remaining stack of orange bills and slapping him across the shoulder with it.

Grandpa continues. "Anyway, I woke up one night to this terrible, terrible pain. It turned out to be Ella, gnawing my arm like it was an ear of corn." He turns to Grandma. "Go ahead. Tell Clint and Rhett what you were dreaming about."

Grandma looks up at the ceiling and scoffs. "Seriously, Henry?"

"Come on. You can't just leave the young'un hanging."

"Fine," she huffs. "I was dreaming about chewing bubblegum."

"Bubblegum?" Rhett asks, scrunching his brows together.

"Yes. Bubblegum."

I look at Rhett. Rhett looks at me. And then we laugh so hard we both fall back in our chairs.

Grandpa stands, taking the last swig from his tea glass. "Well, on that note, I'm going to bed. If my arm is missing tomorrow morning, you boys know what happened."

Grandma slaps him with the cash again. "Hush it."

"I'll hush it when I'm dead," he says.

As Grandpa walks away, Grandma looks at Rhett. "Just ignore him, hon. He's plumb crazy. Me and Clint learned long ago how to tune him out. You will, too."

*You will, too.* I don't like those words. They imply that Rhett isn't going anywhere, that he's here to stay. I sure don't like how she's smiling at him, either, like he's the apple of her eye, even though he just arrived.

My stomach hardens as I look at Rhett again.

Despite what Grandma said earlier about learning to like him and trying to be nice, I can't help but wonder how soon it'll take for her to realize that Rhett doesn't belong here.

# 8
## LIGHTS OUT

"Did you hear that noise?" Rhett asks.

We're in my bedroom. Rhett's on the top bunk. I'm on the bottom. The kid keeps tossing and turning, the squeaking of bedsprings making it impossible for me to go to sleep. He hasn't stopped talking since I shut off the light, either.

"It's just the chickens," I tell him.

"It didn't sound like a chicken."

A few moments later, Sandy's high-pitched yips begin from the front yard.

"The dog is barking," Rhett says.

"Yeah. I know. I have ears."

"Let's go check it out." Rhett's foot hangs down from the top bunk like he's about to climb out of bed and down the ladder. "Sandy could be in trouble. What if she's fighting a grizzly bear? Or a raccoon?"

"It's Florida. We don't have grizzly bears."

"I bet Grandpa has a flashlight we can use."

"We're not waking up Grandpa."

"Well, do you have a flashlight?"

"No. Go to sleep."

I close my eyes.

"What if I get thirsty?" Rhett asks.

I open my eyes. "You won't be thirsty if you go to sleep."

"Can you go with me to get water? What if I fall down the stairs and break my neck? What if I have to go to the bathroom?"

I roll onto my back with a sigh. "Look. You've got to go to sleep. We have school tomorrow."

"School? I'm not going to school."

"Well, I have to. So be quiet."

"Okay."

But the quiet doesn't last for long.

"Clint?"

"What?"

"I think I felt something crawl up my leg. What if it's a roach?"

"It's probably a moth. Or just your imagination. Stop worrying."

I close my eyes again.

But then the bunk above begins to vibrate, rocking back and forth, back and forth. The bedsprings squeal, the sound making me want to cram my ears with tissue paper or place a pillow over my head.

"Hey," I say, gritting my teeth. "Stop shaking the bed."

"I can't."

"Why can't you?"

"I'm bored."

"If you can't get still, then I'm going downstairs to sleep on the couch."

"What? You can't just leave me here all by myself."

"If you don't get quiet, I will."

"Okay. Goodnight."

"Goodnight."

"Clint?"

"Rhett. GO…TO…SLEEP!"

"I will. I just wanted to say something."

"What?" I groan.

"Thank you for letting me stay in here. And your grandparents are really nice. I like them."

"You're welcome. And I know. They're pretty special." *Now hush,* I want to tell him.

"Okay. That's all I wanted to say. Goodnight for real this time."

"Goodnight."

The bed above me continues to vibrate and the springs squeal for another five minutes. Just when I think I can't take it anymore, it stops.

The little rascal is asleep, and I can finally close my eyes.

# 9
## BREAKFAST BRAT

IT'S DAYLIGHT OUTSIDE when I wake up. Aside from the occasional rooster's crow and the whirring ceiling fan overhead, it's quiet, *too* quiet. Rhett must still be asleep.

I decide to let him sleep a little longer while I lay back and think about things.

I think about Bart Kingsley and what he has in store for me today. I think about Rhett's parents and what kind of trouble they might've gotten into and how soon they'll be out of trouble so they can take him back. I think about my list of things I don't like about Rhett, which is probably a little harsh and a little unfair, but it's the truth. I think about Grandma and Grandpa and how a hyperactive seven-year-old can't be good for their health. I wonder: *how long before they realize Rhett has to go?*

After all this thinking, it's still quiet. Even if I strain really hard to hear, I can't even make out the sound of Rhett breathing. With a sigh, I slip out from under my covers and swing my legs over the side of the bed. "Rhett? Are you awake?"

No answer.

My bare feet touch the cold hardwood floor. "Hey, Rhett..."

Still no answer.

Rising on tiptoe, I peek up into the top bunk. My gaze passes over the ruffled sheets, the white pillow, and a blue Scooby-Doo blanket.

No Rhett, which means...

Grandma's shrill laugh sounds from downstairs.

Heat flushes through my body, and my heart pounds. Balling my hands into fists, I stomp all the way across the room and down the stairs. Halfway to the bottom, the smoky smell of bacon wafts into my nostrils.

*That little brat,* I think.

Grandma's voice carries from around the corner, in the dining room. "Now, be a good boy and leave some for Clint."

I step into the dining room, my chest tight.

I hear Rhett before I spot him, bacon crunching between his teeth. He's hunched over the dining room table, elbows resting on the edge, and wearing that same silly, stupid cowboy hat that slips down over his brow.

Grandma notices me first, her silvery-blue eyes meeting mine. "Well, there you are. Were you going to sleep in all morning?"

"You usually call me."

Grandma nods to Rhett across the table, who holds a long piece of bacon in each hand, a sneaky smile forming on his little lips. "Rhett came down all by himself," she says. "I figured you were coming down behind him."

"Well, I figured he was still asleep." My face burns as I look at the little brat hunched over his plate of bacon. "Is there any left for me?"

Grandma leans back with a sigh, holding both of her shoulders. "I think Rhett's cleaned up most of it. You're just going to have to help yourself to a Pop Tart."

"A Pop Tart? I don't even like Pop Tarts!"

Grandma clucks her tongue. "I'm sorry, Clint, but you got up too late. Besides, you're big enough now to get up on your own."

"Yeah, Clint," Rhett whispers, grinning up at me.

I flash him a dirty look.

"I don't have time to cook anything else, either," Grandma says. "I'm taking both of you boys to school this morning."

My stomach clenches. "What? But I want to ride the bus."

Grandma picks at a piece of fuzz on the tablecloth. "Well, you can this afternoon. But I've got to get Rhett enrolled at the elementary school and meet his teacher. I'll drop you off first if that makes you feel better."

"Why do I have to go?"

Grandma shrugs. "I just thought it'd make it easier for Rhett if you tagged along. You boys can chat while I drive us there."

"*You're* driving?" The last time Grandma drove, she took out two mailboxes and ran over a turtle.

"Don't worry. We'll be fine," Grandma says, smiling all the while. "Besides, you can help me watch out for the police."

Since Grandpa's already out plowing the fields, we take his Ram truck, which doesn't have a backseat and forces Rhett to sit between me and Grandma. The AC also doesn't work, so we have to ride with the windows rolled down.

As we're pulling out of the drive, I say a silent prayer that we'll make it to school without incident. After all, riding with Grandma is nothing short of a death wish.

Rhett must notice my bowed head and closed eyes because he asks, "Are you okay, Clint?"

"No."

"What's wrong?"

I open my eyes and turn to look at him. "She's going to kill us," I mouth.

"She's going to do *what*?"

From behind the wheel, Grandma clucks her tongue. "Oh, don't listen to him, Rhett. I've only hit one person."

Rhett's eyes widen. "You hit somebody?"

"Yep. But I didn't kill 'em. They just fell off their bike."

Rhett swallows, and turns back to me. "You're right. We're toast."

"You better hold on," I tell him.

Rhett grips my arm and leans so close his cowboy hat brushes against my shoulder. "I don't like this," he whispers.

"It's okay. Just close your eyes."

"But then I won't be able to see!" says Rhett.

"Well, neither can *she*, so both of you will be even."

Suddenly, Grandma floors the engine, and I'm pinned against the seat, the belt straining against my chest. Wind roars in my ears, coming in through the open windows and tousling my hair.

Grandma squeals as the road twists and the truck rounds a sharp curve at an alarming speed. I grit my teeth, my stomach clenching just like it does on The Scrambler at the county fair.

Rhett presses against me, gripping my arm tighter. When I look down at him, I notice his eyes are pinched shut.

"I don't know about y'all," Grandma yells over the rushing wind, "but I'm having the time of my life!"

# 10

## BART, THE BULLY

On the way to school, Grandma runs two stop signs and one red light. By some miracle, we don't get pulled over by the police. God must have heard my prayers.

"My bad, boys," Grandma says once we're waiting in the drop-off line at the middle school. "These eyes just ain't what they used to be."

"Can I drive next time?" Rhett asks. "Please? That was scary."

"Oh, come on." She pinches his cheek. "You know it was fun."

"Alright," I say, opening the truck door, "I've got to go." When my feet touch the ground, I breathe a big sigh of relief. *We made it.*

"Clint, wait! Don't go. You can't leave me."

When I turn back, Rhett has scooted across the front

seat, sitting on both knees and leaning out the truck door.

"Sorry. You're on your own, kid. I've got to get to class." I close the door before he can hop out, hitch my backpack higher on my shoulders, and walk toward the front door, falling into step behind a couple of other students. Hopefully, I blend in.

As I'm walking away, Grandma yells out through the truck window: "Have a good day, Clint! Make lots of friends. And if you have an emergency, go to the office. They have my number."

I nod my head and give a curt wave, pretending not to notice the girl and boy ahead turning to stare at me, both snickering, just as I pretend not to notice the long line of cars behind Grandma or the one practically on her bumper that keeps edging closer.

"Oh, and eat those beans I packed for you! And pull up those britches. They're sagging."

I turn away, embarrassed, and walk a little faster, hoping, by some miracle, she'll drive off already.

"Love you bunches!" she practically screams, so loud I'm convinced half of the school can hear her.

The couple ahead of me snort with laughter. "Yeah, eat your beans, sonny boy," the girl says, turning to me.

"Dude, that's, like, so embarrassing," the boy says with another snort.

I stare past the couple, pretending to ignore them, just as I pretend to ignore Grandma by not looking back. Maybe if I pretend she doesn't exist, no one else will have any reason to think she's my grandma.

Someone honks in the car line. Once. Twice.

"Go, lady!" a deep voice shouts. "I'm late for work!"

"Ma'am, you're holding up the line," another voice says from the sidewalk.

By the time I make it into the school, my cheeks feel like they're on fire.

Somehow, the day only gets worse.

Before the warning bell, the stern-faced School Resource Officer yells at me to slow down since I'm practically running because Grandma almost made me late. "If I catch you again, I'm sending you to the office," he warns me.

In homeroom, I'm the only person who forgot to get their parent forms signed the night before. It's not like me to forget, but Rhett's arrival yesterday afternoon totally disrupted my world, and if he hadn't shown up, I would have remembered.

In third period, during Language Arts, Ms. Hare (AKA Ms. Cat-hair-sweater) rearranges all of our desks into pods, moving me next to a kid named Jack who should really invest in some deodorant.

During lunch, I scarf down a ham sandwich with far too much mayonnaise, pick at my can of baked beans that would taste much better with bacon, sip on a lukewarm Capri-Sun, and nibble the edge off a dry, rock-like brownie that Grandma left in the oven too long. Even worse is that several drops of brown baked bean sauce drip onto my white T-shirt. Scrubbing my shirt with a napkin only makes the stains worse.

At P.E., Coach Davis won't let me play basketball with the other kids since I'm wearing sandals. Instead, I have to walk laps around the gym.

In seventh period, Bart Kingsley is the final nail in the coffin. When he's not kicking the back of my chair, he's mumbling snide remarks under his breath.

*"What's that mess on your shirt? First time feeding yourself, baby?"*

*"Nice shoes. Did you get them at the church yard sale?"*

*"I bet your hair's so short 'cause you can't get rid of lice. Right, Cowgirl?"*

I do my best to ignore him.

Once the bell finally rings, I gather my things and hurry out the door. I don't look back once to see if Bart's following. Maybe if I pretend he doesn't exist, he will leave me alone.

I'm ten steps away from the school bus when there's a tug on the back of my sandal. Then I hear a loud pop. The next thing I know I'm on the ground, my palms and knees digging into the hot asphalt. A shadow falls over me, and I look up.

It's Bart, smiling like he didn't just step on the back of my sandal and cause me to trip. "Thought you could get away from me, Cowgirl?" he laughs, a bit of his spittle landing on my cheek. He leans closer, his voice turning into a snarl. "Looks like you're gonna have to get another pair of those Jerusalem sandals." He straightens his shoulders and walks away. I stare after him, my palms and knees stinging as anger tightens in my chest and I try not to cry.

My broken sandal lies a few feet away on the scorching-hot pavement.

Before I can bother to reach it, a familiar voice sounds above me. "Hey. You alright?"

I look up again. It's Aaliyah. She stares down at me with wide eyes.

"Yeah, I'm okay," I tell her, rising to my feet. "Just tripped."

"You sure about that?" she asks as I pick up my sandal. Her gaze falls to my skinned knees, oozing blood.

I pretend not to hear her.

Broken sandal in hand now, I limp toward the bus, also pretending not to notice the crowd of people several feet away, watching us.

Aaliyah turns to them and shouts, "You fools never seen someone trip before? Don't act like you've never done it."

I might've laughed if I weren't so embarrassed.

Climbing the bus steps, my throat tightens, and tears burn the backs of my eyes. *You will not cry,* I tell myself. *Crying is for wimps.*

I barely make it two steps down the aisle before I notice the little boy sitting alone in the second row, staring up at me. The surprised look on his face tells me he watched the entire scene from the bus window.

Great. Now *he's* here, which means I can't sit with Aaliyah. Which means I have to make him promise he won't tell Grandma what he just saw.

*Can this day get any worse?* I think.

Rhett's eyes widen as I plop down beside him. "Are you okay?" he asks.

I look at him and hope he can't notice the tears forming in my eyes, the ones I do my best to blink away. "Does it look like I'm okay?"

It's the first time I've seen him without the cowboy hat. His hair is black, just like mine, but a little longer and curlier. He could easily pass for my brother. Honestly, I'm not quite sure how that makes me feel.

"I saw that," Rhett says.

"Saw what?"

"That kid. He tripped you."

"Oh, that was nothing." I hope he'll believe me. "He was just messing around."

Rhett frowns. "No, he wasn't. You should trip him back!" His gaze falls to my feet. "But you're going to have to get a better pair of shoes than that."

"What? No, Rhett. I'm not tripping him."

"Why? Are you scared?"

It's not above me that a seven-year-old's asking if *I'm* the one who's scared. On that note, I change the subject. "How was school?"

But Rhett isn't having it. "Sure you're okay?" he asks again.

"Of course I am."

Pretty soon, Aaliyah's back, sitting in the row across from us. I tell her I'm fine, that it's nothing, that it was just an accident. Then I introduce her to Rhett, tell her he's my grandma's cousin, and that he will be staying with us for a while.

"Well, it's obvious he's a relative, 'cause he looks just like you, Clint," says Aaliyah. "Are you up for a little brother?"

"I don't have a choice."

She lowers her voice. "Trust me: it's rough."

"Tell me about it."

"One might not be that bad. At least you don't have six."

Rhett leans across my lap and says, "Are you Clint's girlfriend?"

Aaliyah tosses her head back and laughs. I flash Rhett a dirty look.

After a few minutes, and after Aaliyah makes me chuckle and helps cheer me up, I start to feel a little better. The entire bus ride home, I can't pretend not to notice the serious look on Rhett's face or that mischievous glint in his eye. Even if I've only known him for a little less than twenty-four hours, that look tells me he's up to something. Whatever it is, it can't be good.

# 11

## PEA PICKIN' PRO

When I get home, I tell Grandma I broke my sandal after getting it hung on the edge of the sidewalk. She just shakes her head and mumbles, "'Course you did."

Thankfully, that's all she has to say about it. While I do feel guilty about lying to her, I don't want her to worry about someone bullying me at school. This is my problem; it shouldn't also be hers.

After pouring hydrogen peroxide on my bloody palms and skinned knees, she bandages me up, and even gives me a pair of her black rubber boots to wear while I complete my chores.

All the while, Rhett watches with a confused look on his face. He's probably wondering why I don't just tell her the truth, but I can't, or else Bart will find out somehow and do far worse than step on the back of my sandal. Still, I am somewhat surprised that he doesn't snitch. Then again, I barely know him. Maybe he's not like that.

Once I've fed the chickens, gathered the eggs, taken out the trash, and retrieved the mail from the mailbox, I join Grandma and Rhett in the garden for the final chore of the day: pea-picking. To me, it's easy, mindless work. The only bad thing about it is the Florida heat, which is almost unbearable, both sweltering and persistent. As Grandpa would say, it's hotter'n a blister bug in a pea patch.

Fat droplets of sweat drip down my face as I squat to the ground and search for the long green pea pods hiding amid plant leaves. I pick the most mature ones, which are fat and firm, tossing them in a large plastic bucket; I have to use my fingers mostly, since my palms are bandaged up.

While Rhett works with Grandma several rows over, I listen to her explain how to spot for peas and know which ones to pick. It's the same thing she taught me when I was seven, back before I had to worry about bullies like Bart Kingsley or children like Rhett who disrupt your life in the blink of an eye, changing everything.

"You'll be a little pea-pickin' pro before you know it," she tells him.

I should feel happy for Rhett, now that he's been given a better chance, but selfishly, envy grows in my chest. After all, those are the same words she said to me when I was his age—ones I never imagined I'd hear her say to anyone else. For as long as I can remember, it's always been me and Grandma, working side-by-side through the rows, telling stories and laughing until our buckets are filled with peas.

I never thought I'd be this…replaceable. I never thought that when I would need my grandparents the most, they'd devote all of their attention to someone else. But I guess that's the cruel reality of change, how quickly it can wrap its fingers around your life and snatch away everything safe and familiar.

*Change is a part of life,* Grandpa always says. But if it wasn't, I imagine things would be a whole lot better than they are now. Without change, maybe I wouldn't have to worry about people like Bart Kingsley making fun of my haircut or stepping on the back of my sandal. Maybe I wouldn't have to worry about Rhett taking my place, requiring more of my grandparents' attention than I expected. Maybe I wouldn't have to worry about a new school with new people, or how difficult it is for me to fit in. Without change, maybe I wouldn't feel so alone.

For what seems like hours, I pick and toss, pick and toss, until my bucket's almost full, my legs sore from so much squatting. Every laugh from Rhett and Grandma is as unbearable as the heat and humidity, which is so thick and heavy that I'd love nothing more than to stick my head in the freezer or pour a cold glass of water down my neck to cool me down. Before long, Grandpa walks through the rickety garden gate and joins me, going on and on about some deer stand he wants to put up, but I only half-hear him; I'm too busy thinking about how miserable my life has become.

"Clint." Grandpa says my name sharp enough to

make my thoughts trail away. "Did you hear anything I just said?"

"I'm sorry, Grandpa. I've got a lot on my mind."

"Is it a girl?"

"What? No!" I snatch a pod from its vine and throw it into the bucket, annoyed.

"Is it school? How's that been goin' for ya?"

*Oh, so now you care?* I think.

"Fine," I mumble.

"Doesn't seem like it." Grandpa stops picking and turns to face me. Sweat drips from the end of his nose onto the dirt. "Something I should know about?"

I look down and don't answer.

"Clint? What's gotten into you?"

That's all it takes for me to break. "Nothing. Everything's great! I have soooo many friends, I love allll my teachers, and I just looove that I basically have a new brother that no one bothered to give me a heads-up about and the fact that no one cared to ask how I've been for two whole days. Everything's great!" I turn to face him. My cheeks burn, but not because of the heat. "Is that what you want me to say?"

Grandpa blinks several times. Then he goes back to picking. "Well," he says, "sounds like someone's hormones are out of whack."

"No, they're not. I'm perfectly fine."

Grandpa wipes the sweat off his forehead. "Sounds like a hormone problem to me."

"What do you suggest I do about it?" My tone sounds sarcastic and whiny, but I don't care.

"Go hit something. Go punch a tree. That'll take your mind off things."

"Punch a tree? Are you serious? I'll break my hand!"

"I'm serious as all get out. When your great Aunt Theresa was a young'un, she'd come home from school madder than a puffed toad. I figured it was either hormones or the kids teasing her about her twiddling…you know, that nervous habit of hers where she twists and twirls her hair or a handkerchief or a pillowcase between her fingertips. Anyways, she had to get her anger out somehow, so Daddy bought her a punching bag. You need a punching bag, Clint?"

I stand up. "I want to stop. I want to go back to the house."

Grandpa doesn't answer; he just continues picking peas, a slight smile tugging at his lips.

"I want to go to my room *right now*."

"Then go. Nobody's stopping you."

Grandpa's response is flat, too nonchalant. It's not what I expect. He's never treated me like this before, like I'm this insignificant. "Well, are you goin' or are you just gonna stand there?"

His words make me come to my senses: I'm acting like a brat. A spoiled, selfish brat. For once, he's treating me as such. "I'm sorry. I-I didn't mean any of that. It just…slipped."

"Don't worry about it," Grandpa says. "I've been there a few times myself."

I drop down into a squat and start picking through the pea pods again. Beside me, Grandpa begins to whistle "Hey, Good Lookin'."

When I look up a moment later, I notice Grandma and Rhett a couple rows over now, watching me. It doesn't take long for me to realize they must've heard my every word. My face, neck, and ears feel impossibly hot.

Rather than acknowledge my tantrum, Grandma straightens and claps her hands together. My eyes lock onto the red bandanna tied around her forehead. She always wears it on hot, humid afternoons like this to keep the sweat from dripping into her eyes. "Alright, boys," she says. "How about a pea-pickin' contest?"

"Yes!" says Rhett. "That sounds fun."

"Clint?"

"Sure," I mumble.

"First, I need you boys to go get four buckets from out of the shed. Then we'll get started."

Without another word, we do as she says.

"Race you there!" Rhett calls to me, sprinting out of the garden to the rusty tin-roofed shed in the corner of the backyard. I don't bother running after him.

As I trudge away, I hear Grandma ask, "What was that about?"

"It's all startin' to get to him, I reckon," Grandpa says.

When I make it to the shed, Rhett's already found the buckets. He tries balancing one on his head.

"Are you okay?" Rhett asks me, just as the bucket clatters onto the dusty shed floor. "Sounded like you were upset."

I don't answer him; I simply grab the other two buckets and head back to the garden.

Rhett passes me on the way, holding the buckets

by their silver handle, swinging them by his sides. At one point, he stops, sets one bucket on the ground, and throws the other one straight up into the air, holding his hands out to catch it.

I roll my eyes. The kid has more energy than sense.

Back at the garden, we each get a bucket and our own row of peas. Grandpa counts us off, and then we begin, snatching pods between our fingers and tossing them into our buckets as fast as we can. Snatch. Toss. Repeat.

Maybe it's due to anger, frustration, or a bit of both, but soon, my bucket's halfway full, and I barely notice the throbbing of my sore, cut-up hands. Salty sweat trickles into my mouth, stings the corners of my eyes. My back aches from so much stooping over. I wonder if this is how Grandma and Grandpa feel on a daily basis.

At some point, I stop to catch my breath. After all, I can afford the break; I'm fairly certain I'm way ahead of the others.

Beyond the garden, heat shimmers in the distant fields. Several dairy cows graze in the pale-green pastures, others lie in the sparse shade of the occasional oak tree, chewing their cud and staring in our direction. I stare back. All the while, cicadas sing from the trees, a sound that I used to think was the sizzling heat on a summer day. For a moment, I close my eyes, the insects' familiar buzzing calming my racing heart.

I'm about to resume picking when Grandma yells out, "Done!"

"What?" Rhett looks up, his face as red as a tomato. "How?"

"'Cause she cheated," Grandpa says. His blue work shirt is so soaked through with sweat that it looks as though he just jumped into the creek. "That's how."

"I didn't cheat, Henry! I'm just on a goldmine over here."

"Ella, there is no possible way you've out-picked these boys."

"Hush up, and come look."

So we do.

Sure enough, Grandma's right—her bucket is filled to the brim with green pea pods.

"No way," Grandpa whispers.

"That's it. I give up," I groan.

"Wait," Rhett says, "that's the same bucket you were using before we started our contest! You *did* cheat!"

Grandma places her hands on her hips. "Y'all are some sore losers," she says, shaking her head.

"But we didn't lose!" Rhett shouts. "*You* cheated!"

"Don't know what you're talkin' about. Now let's take these buckets inside and get washed up for supper."

Rhett kicks at the dirt. "That's no fair!"

"Life's not fair, hon," Grandma says. Then she looks at Grandpa and winks.

# 12
## MEMORIES

For the second night in a row, I eat my dinner without speaking a single word. I halfway hear the others as they joke and laugh and ask Rhett about his first day of school, and I halfway hear the TV later when we're all sitting in the living room, watching some western Grandpa's seen at least a hundred times.

I'm reminded of my first several days here after my parents died, when I choked down my food and watched my cartoons in bitter silence, feeling more alone with every second that passed without Mom and Dad. It wasn't long before my worrying reached a new peak. I worried the same thing that had happened to my parents would happen to Grandma and Grandpa, and then I would have no one. I worried that I would never again feel loved or happy. I worried that I would always feel alone.

Even at six years old, I was a nervous wreck.

Back then, change had snatched away the two most important people in my life, dumping me on a farm with a grandma and grandpa I wasn't as familiar and comfortable with as my parents. It didn't make sense how things had turned out. Everything felt pointless, kind of like how life feels now.

Honestly, my parents' deaths made just as much sense then as Rhett's arrival does now. If change is so necessary, why does it come during the most unexpected moments? Why can't it at least give me a heads-up before ruining my life? Wouldn't I be more prepared? Wouldn't that make more sense?

Later that night, these questions pass through my mind as I'm trying to fall asleep. While counting sheep typically works for me every time, tonight even that doesn't do the trick.

My bedsprings creak as I roll over onto my side for what feels like the fiftieth time, trying to get comfortable. A moment later, Rhett's voice sounds from the top bunk.

"Hey, Clint?" he whispers.

"Yeah?"

"I can't sleep."

"Me either."

I shift onto my back, staring up toward the ceiling. Thinking aloud, I say, "Do you ever feel like life isn't fair?"

Rhett is silent for a beat. "What do you mean?"

"I mean, I don't understand why this had to happen to me or why my parents had to leave. I feel like...like I've been left behind."

"I don't understand, either," says Rhett.

Of course he doesn't; I shouldn't expect him to. He's only seven.

"I thought Grandma and Grandpa were your parents," he says.

"No. Not technically."

"Then where are your *real* Mom and Dad? Why don't they ever come to see you?"

The question hits me like a gut punch. My voice cracks as I whisper, "They're not here anymore."

"What do you mean?"

"I mean they're gone. They passed away when I was six."

"Oh. I'm sorry."

"It's okay." I take a deep breath. "What about your parents? What happened to them?"

"They're in jail, probably," Rhett says, matter-of-fact.

"Really? For what?"

"They're always fighting. And they scream a lot. And sometimes they forget that I'm there."

"Do they ever hurt each other?"

"Yeah," he says, after a long pause.

"Well, I'm sorry you had to see that."

"I got used to it," says Rhett.

"It probably is confusing, why you had to come here."

"No, it's not. I came here because I needed a new home."

"Me too," I say. "After my parents died, I had nowhere else to go."

"I like this place better anyway. Everyone's really nice. And the food is good, too."

I chuckle. "You haven't had Grandma's pork chops. They're harder to chew than leather."

"Yuck!"

*Maybe Rhett was meant to be here*, I think, *even if I don't know why yet.*

Although I doubt I'll get the answer to that anytime soon.

"How'd your parents die?" he asks.

"Car wreck."

"Oh. Do you miss them?"

"Always." I take another deep breath. "After they died, I felt like I was sinking. All the time. Sort of like my insides were all tangled up. Even breathing was hard." A lump forms in my throat, but I continue. "Grandma calls that feeling grief. She said it's normal to feel that way after losing someone you love, but it didn't feel normal. It felt like I was sick."

Sometimes, I still feel that way. In fact, I miss them so much it feels like my chest is going to cave in sometimes. In my head, my parents are still alive. And sometimes, when I close my eyes and think about them, I shock myself with how much I remember.

Tonight, I remember how Mom would come into my room, kiss me on the forehead, and sing me a song to put me to sleep. I remember playing human stilts with Dad, which consisted of me stepping on his feet and him walking around, carrying me around the yard. He never let me fall, not once.

I remember watching movies with Mom and teasing her about crying at the simplest things. She could never make it through a movie without shedding a tear. I remember playing basketball with Dad, and how I was never good enough to beat him, even though he let me win a few times. And I remember snuggling up next to them with a book as they read to me, pointed at the pictures, and exclaimed when they turned the pages; I never felt so safe and loved as when I was being read to.

If they were still here today, who knows how many more memories we would have. For some reason, they had to go, and they couldn't take me with them.

It's not fair. It just seems…pointless.

Rhett's voice interrupts my thoughts. "I always get on my parents' nerves."

*I don't doubt that,* I think.

"What about you?" I ask him. "Do you miss your parents?"

"A little. But I don't think they miss me." A pause. "I don't want to go back there."

My chest tightens with guilt…guilt for ever wanting him to leave. His parents don't sound like good people. Something tells me they didn't kiss him goodnight and sing him to sleep. Something tells me they didn't read to him and make him feel safe and loved. I don't even want to think about what might've happened if he continued to live with them. At least here, Grandma and Grandpa will make sure he's loved and fed and gets a good night's sleep.

"Hey, Clint? You still awake?"

"Yeah. Just thinking."

"About what?"

"You wouldn't understand."

"Why? I'm almost eight, you know. I'm not a baby." Rhett's sheets rustle, and he lets out a long yawn. "Okay, whatever. Goodnight. I'm going to see if I can sleep now."

"Goodnight, Rhett."

I've barely closed my eyes when I hear him whisper, "Clint?"

"Yeah?" I whisper back.

"Are your hands and knees still sore?"

"A little."

"Well, I'm glad you're okay."

My throat aches, but I'm not sure why.

"I'm really glad you're here," Rhett adds.

The words escape before I can stop them. "I'm glad you're here, too."

# *13*

## BUS BRAWL

AFTER THREE DAYS of middle school, it's safe to say I don't think I belong here. I think it's just me, because everyone else seems to be getting along just fine. Everyone sort of looks the same too, with their white Vans, their long, styled hair, and brand-name T-shirts.

Then there's me: the kid with the cowboy name, a horrid military buzz cut, and his grandma's black rubber boots. Until now, I've never been more embarrassed to be myself.

At least in elementary school the teachers acted like they cared about me. They even ate lunch with me sometimes, so I had no reason to feel alone. My fifth-grade teacher, Mrs. Douglass, even brought me a Snickers bar that one time, which I thought was really nice.

Here, the teachers seem much more interested in their

coffees, their phones, or their watches. They always look bored and miserable, which is what I imagine I must look like all the time in math class.

Another thing I've had to get used to is how easy it is for everyone to act like I don't exist. Sometimes at PE or at lunch, I sit and watch the others, waiting for them to look my way, but they never do. How is it possible to feel so lonesome in a room full of people?

Whenever I get so lonesome that my chest starts to ache, I open a book and read. I've found that reading cures nearly everything: boredom, loneliness, even anger. What's great about books is that they're reliable; they're safe. Life changes, but the words in the books stay the same.

Sometimes, when I'm reading, my thoughts drift to Rhett. Honestly, I've been thinking more about him lately. I wonder if he's having the same problems at school. After all, I don't know many kids who wear a cowboy hat.

I think about Aaliyah too, and how much easier middle school might be if only I had her to talk to. But she's in seventh grade, so I doubt she'd even want to talk to me in the first place. She probably has a ton of friends who are way cooler than me. I guess should be thankful that I get to spend every morning and afternoon with her on the bus, even if that's nowhere near enough.

I also don't know how to tell her about Bart. Sure, he might be the only person who dares speak to me, but he's a nuisance and a curse. How Bart keeps any friends around is beyond me.

Seventh period is more of the same—Bart kicking

my chair whenever Ms. Flynn isn't watching, mumbling *Cowgirl* and other snide comments under his breath, and tossing paper airplanes at my back. Once the bell rings, I'm sprinting for the door, foolish enough to think I can get away this time, that I can make it on the bus before he can terrorize me anymore. Just like yesterday, and the day before that, Bart lingers like a shadow, lengthening his stride every time I manage to speed up.

He finally catches me as I'm about to board the bus. "Where ya think you're going, Cowgirl?" he hisses, one hand gripping my elbow.

"Let me go." I try to tug away, but Bart's grip tightens.

"Not so fast, *Clint*." My name sounds vile and rotten in his mouth.

Turning to face him, I notice those big, pale lips of his are pulled back in a hideous, yellow-toothed smile.

"Worthless piece of trash," he says, his hot spittle spraying my face, my neck.

I blink up at him. "Bart, seriously, knock it off."

He bends down until we're eye-level. "Bart, seriously, knock it off," he mocks, raising his voice several octaves higher.

I take a deep breath, close my eyes, and then open them again.

Before I can think better of it, I kick Bart in the shin.

He stumbles back, and his grip on my elbow loosens. "You little piece of—"

But I don't hear the rest; I've already bolted away, up the bus steps.

Standing in the center aisle, blocking my path, is Rhett. "I saw that," he says.

"Move! He's coming."

Rhett doesn't budge. "Go sit down, Clint. I've got this."

Before I can ask what that means, the bus trembles beneath my feet. Heart pounding, I look back over my shoulder.

Bart is tromping up the steps and down the aisle. His large eyes are locked on mine. "You shouldn't have done that, Cowgirl," he snarls.

My first instinct is to run, but I have nowhere to go—nearly all the seats are taken up by students. For once, some of them are even staring at me.

A hand digs into my side—Rhett, pushing past.

"*Hey.*" Rhett stares up at Bart, his tiny hands balled into fists.

*Oh no,* I think. *Rhett, don't—*

I'm too late. In the blink of an eye, Rhett rears his boot back and kicks Bart straight between the legs.

First, Bart's grimace morphs into a look of surprise, his mouth forming a small O. Then he moans, falling to his knees.

Rhett just keeps kicking. His pointed boots strike Bart's side, his stomach, his groin with a sound like a wooden bat striking a baseball. Rhett even raises one of his fists and swings.

"Stop that!" I shout, lifting him under the arms and pulling him off Bart, my heart racing.

I fall back on to the closest seat as Rhett continues to swing his fists and kick with his heels, striking nothing but air. "Enough!" I hiss into his ear.

Soon, Rhett's small body goes slack.

"Did I get him?" he asks, breathless.

"Yeah," I say. "You definitely got him."

He slides off my lap and onto the vinyl seat, brushing several strands of black hair out of his eyes. "He shouldn't bother you anymore."

Heart still pounding, I look toward the front of the bus—past Bart, who's slowly rising to his feet—and at the small mirror above where the bus driver sits. The driver isn't even watching; he's staring down at his phone, earplugs in, head bobbing to his music.

Behind us, I hear the excited whispers from the others.

"Oh my God. Someone please tell me you videoed that!"

"That dude fell harder than a sack of rocks!"

"You think he's alright?"

"He doesn't look alright."

"Should we go help?"

"No way. That little kid took care of business."

I lean back against my seat. Close my eyes. Take a deep breath.

"Are you okay?"

I crack an eye open. *Aaliyah.*

She stands in the center aisle, holding out her hand to Bart, who's currently bent at the waist, his hands clutching his privates, breaths shaky and labored. "Does it look like I'm okay?"

Aaliyah drops her hand and places it on her hip. "Geez, dude. Lose the 'tude. I'm just asking!" She rolls her eyes. Then she notices me, tilting her head to the side. "Clint, do you know what just happened here?"

I open my mouth to speak but Rhett beats me to

it. "You missed it," he says. "You should've been here. That guy was beatin' up on Clint, so I took care of it."

Aaliyah frowns. "What? You mean—"

She looks back and forth between Rhett and Bart, understanding finally crossing her face.

"Just leave him alone and come sit down. He'll be okay," I tell her.

Squeezing past Bart, she sits down in the row across from us. "Beating up on you? Clint, what is going on?"

I sigh, pinching the bridge of my nose. "It's been one heck of a week, if you can't tell."

"Oh my God," Aaliyah says. "And you haven't said anything?"

"I didn't want you to worry."

"So? It's better than not telling anyone." Her brown eyes settle on Rhett. "And you're lucky the bus driver doesn't write you up."

Rhett shrugs and clucks his tongue. "Let him. I don't care. I've been in trouble before."

I thump Rhett's shoulder.

"What?" he says.

"Enough."

He huffs and looks out the window.

"So, when did this start?" Aaliyah's looking straight at me now, brows furrowed.

My gaze falls to my lap. "You don't want to know."

"Seriously, Clint? I thought we were friends."

I look up. "We are."

*You're my only friend,* I almost say, but I bite the words back.

Aaliyah folds her arms. "Well, it doesn't seem like it.

Not when you refuse to tell me what's going on. If someone's hurting you, you've got to say something."

"Say what? No one cares, Aaliyah."

"*I* care."

"Yeah," Rhett says. "So do I."

The knot in my chest loosens, like a weight's been lifted off of me. "Thank you," I whisper, but it's so soft, I doubt they even hear it.

Besides, Aaliyah's too focused on Bart, who finally staggers past, his lips pinched together and his chin lowered to his chest, too ashamed to even make eye contact. "That's right, keep walking," she mutters to his back.

Out of the corner of my eye, I notice Rhett tense beside me, his hands balling into fists again. I reach out and squeeze his knee, letting him know I'm okay.

Once Bart's gone, Aaliyah shakes her head and says, "What a turd! Why would anyone want to hurt you anyway? You're so…"

"So what?" I ask.

"Kind," Aaliyah says. "There aren't too many kind people around here."

I rub the raw place on my palm from where my hand scraped the pavement yesterday. "I guess being kind doesn't matter so much in middle school," I say. "It's not really that cool."

"Being kind matters. Period," Aaliyah says.

"Well, maybe you're right."

"I'm *always* right, Clint. Let's get that straight." She laughs, and I start laughing too.

"Hey," Rhett says beside me. "What do you think Grandma's making for dinner?"

"Woah, buddy, not so fast. Let's not forget what you just did." I poke him in the ribs. "You know you shouldn't have done that."

Rhett shrugs again. "I wanted to."

"You wanted to beat someone up? Why? That's not okay."

"Because," Rhett says, "you're my brother."

# *14*
# CUCUMBERS & KUMQUATS

LATER THAT AFTERNOON, after finishing my chores, I begin my homework.

First up is math. It's my least favorite subject, so I want to get it over with as soon as possible.

I lay out all my materials on the dining room table—a couple of pencils in case one of them breaks, a sheet of notebook paper, a calculator, and my math workbook. Grandma's called me both a neat freak and a perfectionist for as long as I can remember, which I guess is a good thing because my grades are always above average.

I've just started my fifth word problem when Rhett pulls up a chair beside me.

"Watcha doin'?" he says.

"Homework."

"Can I watch?"

"Don't you have schoolwork to do?"

"No."

"Lucky," I mumble.

"So can I watch?"

"As long as you're quiet. I'm trying to concentrate."

"Okay," Rhett says.

I read the math word problem once, twice, and then underline the key words.

Rhett props an elbow on my shoulder. "Can you hurry up? I'm bored."

"Shhh! I just started."

"Well, it's taking you forever."

"Sorry. Go watch TV or something. I'm going to be here for a while."

Rhett looks down at my workbook. "Why can't I help you?"

I sigh, skimming a hand over my hair. "Because," I tell him, "you won't understand it. This is too hard for a seven-year-old."

Rhett folds his arms across his tiny chest and raises his chin. "I bet it's easy. You're just slow."

"Okay, then." I slide the book in front of him and point at the problem. "*You* read it. Tell me what you think I should do."

"Alright," Rhett says.

He stares at it for a minute. Then he begins to read. "Tiff-a-ny has six-ty—"

"Sixty-four."

Rhett looks at me. "I know. You didn't let me finish."

"My bad. Go on."

Rhett sighs. "Where was I?"

"Sixty-four," I say again.

Rhett takes a deep breath and starts back. "Tiffany has sixty-four kumquats—"

"Cucumbers."

"That's what I said!"

I press my palms to my eyes. "Just keep going."

"She dividends them—"

"*Divides* them."

"Whatever." He slides the book back over to me, slumping in his chair. "This is boring. Can we do something else?"

Before I can tell him to hush and leave me alone, Grandma steps around the corner. "Watcha boys workin' on?" she asks, both hands on her hips, her red bandanna tied around her forehead.

"Homework," I say with a sigh.

"And I'm helping," Rhett adds.

Grandma smiles. "I don't doubt it. You boys need my assistance?"

"We're good," I tell her.

"No, Grandma, he's not. Clint can barely read!"

"Yeah right." I roll my eyes. "Coming from the one who said kumquats instead of cucumbers…"

"Boys," Grandma says, "stop bickering. You're probably both wrong." She walks over and takes a seat at the table. "Give me that book. Let me see what all the fuss is about."

I do as she says. "Problem number five," I tell her.

Grandma pushes her glasses farther up her nose. Then she places a finger beneath the first word of the problem. "Alright. Here we go." She clears her throat. "Tiffany has sixty-four cucumbers—"

I thump Rhett's shoulder. "See? I told you it didn't say kumquats."

Rhett sticks his tongue out at me.

Grandma frowns. "Why does Tiffany have sixty-four cucumbers in the first place?"

"Sounds like Tiffany's got herself in a pickle," Grandpa shouts from the living room.

"You got that right." Grandma licks her lips and starts again. "She divides them into four equal piles. How many cucumbers does Tiffany have in two piles?"

"Oh, that's easy," Rhett says.

"Hush it," Grandma says back. "I'm trying to focus."

I pick up my pencil and start writing on the notebook paper. First, I divide sixty-four by four, which equals sixteen. Then I multiply sixteen by two. "I know the answer," I tell her.

"Yeah?" Grandma keeps staring down at the book. "And what is it?"

"Thirty-two. Tiffany has thirty-two cucumbers in two piles."

Grandma looks up. "How'd you figure that out so fast?"

"Here. Look at this." I pass over the paper.

Grandma adjusts her glasses again. Eyes squinted, brows furrowed, and her mouth slightly agape, she examines my work. "That's how y'all do it now?"

"Pretty much."

"Shoot. Teachers these days don't have enough sense to pour pee out of a boot with the directions written on the heel. Here, let me show you how I learned it." She takes my pencil and starts working out the problem.

"Lord help us," Rhett whispers to me. "We're doomed."

Grandma stops writing and looks at him. "What'd you say, young man?"

Rhett flashes a toothy grin. "Nothing, Grandma."

"That's what I thought."

Next door, in the living room, I hear the clip-clop of horse's hooves, then the *Jeopardy* theme song, and then gunfire.

It's Grandpa, flipping through the channels. He always does that, even though he always ends up watching *Gunsmoke* or *The Lone Ranger*.

After a minute, he says, "You boys sure are desperate if you're needin' Ella's help. She barely made it to the eighth grade, ya know."

If Grandma hears him, she doesn't say anything. Instead, she tucks the pencil behind her ear and points to the sheet of paper. "This is how you do it. C'mere, Clint, and get a good look."

So I do. But Grandma's work looks like nonsense, a jumble of numbers, letters, and random pencil marks. The longer I look at it, the less sense it makes. "Where's your answer?" I ask. "And what are all of those marks for?"

"It's right here. The answer is sixteen. And each of these little marks are cucumbers."

"Grandma, those look like little worms," Rhett says with a frown.

From the living room, Grandpa shouts, "Well, maybe Tiffany's got worms in her cucumbers."

"What?" I put a palm to my face. "Now I'm just confused."

"Well, let's try another one," Grandma says.

"Try problem number six."

Grandma puts a finger beneath each word as she reads. "Greg has one hundred and twenty balloons…"

All of a sudden, Grandma shuts the book and stands up. "Forget it," she says. "This is worthless! It doesn't even make good sense. What need do two people have for so many kumquats and balloons?"

"Cucumbers, not kumquats," I tell her.

"Oh, same difference!" She starts walking toward the living room.

"Wait, so that's it? You give up?"

"Son," she says, turning to face me with a hand on her hip, "I'd rather watch the news. At least the weatherman's cute."

Rhett gasps beside me. "Grandma!"

Grandma chuckles. "I mean it. I'd sop him up with a biscuit."

"Ewww!" Rhett gags and holds his stomach. "I think I'm gonna be sick."

I look back down at my math book. *Only five more problems to go,* I think.

Then I notice Rhett, standing at the edge of the table, glancing between me and the living room, as if he can't make up his mind, not knowing whether to stay or leave me be.

I think about what he did earlier this afternoon, kicking Bart with his pointed cowboy boots. Turning to me and saying, "He shouldn't bother you anymore."

At that moment, I realize what I have to do.

I push the book away. "Hey, how about we go outside? Maybe throw a little football? Shoot my new bow Grandpa got me for Christmas?"

Rhett's eyes widen. "Really? But I thought you were too busy."

"I thought I was," I tell him. "But it can wait."

# *15*

# THE TALK

Bart doesn't bother me the next day. Or the day after that. While I'm still not comfortable with middle school, him not calling me names or throwing paper airplanes at my back makes it a tad more tolerable.

Rhett and I keep what happened on the bus a secret from our grandparents. We don't talk about it, but I like to think the incident brought us a little bit closer. Instead, we talk about other stuff, like possibly going to the Choctawhatchee River sometime to fish or helping Grandpa with his new deer stand. I've even started helping Rhett with his homework.

Friday night, I'm worn slap out after my first full week of middle school and end up falling asleep on the couch. Grandma wakes me up at some point, watching me walk groggily up the stairs to my room before turning the lights out.

Saturday morning, I wake way earlier than usual, full of energy the moment my feet touch the hardwood floor. Rhett's gentle snores drift down from the top bunk. I'm careful not to wake him.

Downstairs, Grandma's already up and about, pouring a bowl of egg yolk into a skillet on the kitchen stove.

"Good morning," I tell her.

"Your grandpa's on the porch." She stares down at the sizzling skillet. "He wants to talk to you."

"Right now?"

"Yes, Clint. Right now." She looks at me over her shoulder. "Don't worry. You're not in trouble."

"Then what does he want to talk about?"

"I don't know, but go on out there. Breakfast will be ready soon."

With a sigh, I do as Grandma says.

Outside, Grandpa is sitting on the porch swing, the metal links creaking as he rocks back and forth. His brow is furrowed, his bottom lip poked out. He looks serious. "Clint," he says, when the door slips shut behind me, "come sit. There's something I've got to tell you."

*If this is about the birds and the bees, I'll throw up,* I think.

Once I'm seated beside him on the swing, Grandpa clasps his hands behind his head and says, "I decided you're old enough now for me to tell you the rest about 'Nam."

"Oh," I say. "Alright."

He picks up from where he left off the last time we

talked, after he was drafted at eighteen and had to leave his family and Mossy Bend behind. "We were just boys in men's uniforms, playing in the government's wicked game," he says. "You can't judge any of us too hard for trying or blame any of the people in 'Nam who fought against us. 'Course, we were both fighting for the same thing."

"What same thing?"

"Our lives," he says. "We found out real quick that no one wins in war."

He goes on to describe how after a year of combat, his unit landed in Washington D.C. to an angry crowd of protestors.

"They laughed at us, spit at us, and called us names," he says, referring to the swarm of anti-war activists. "Told us we weren't welcome here, as if we had a choice whether to fight or not. As if it wasn't politics that sent us to war in the first place. After all we did for this country, it wasn't enough for those people."

"Why would they do that?"

"They didn't like that we were fighting in 'Nam in the first place. They called us monsters...made it plain and clear they didn't like us being at war. I'd never seen war protests before, 'cept for on TV. I found out later it wasn't just me personally they didn't like, but anyone in the green uniform or in the administration. It beat all I'd ever seen."

"What administration?"

"President Johnson. Lyndon Baines Johnson. He's the one who sent us over there."

"Well," I say, looking down at my threadbare socks,

"I would've been proud of you. You're a hero. You did the right thing."

"Son, there's nothing right about war. Nothing good ever comes of it. And I'm no hero. Anyone who rallies for war, for so many guns in men's hands, has never stood shivering in his boots in the middle of a battlefield. And anyone who fights simply to be a man ain't a man. He doesn't have enough compassion."

I start to understand then. Maybe it's war that makes Grandpa look sad sometimes. Maybe it's the thought that it can happen at any moment or the thought that there will always be war that makes him appear melancholy, like on those afternoons he sits stone-faced in his recliner while Hank Williams' lonesome voice fills the house, singing of the blue whippoorwill and the weeping robin. Maybe Grandpa wants me to realize that being a soldier doesn't make someone a hero or a man, but having compassion does.

Grandpa goes on. "In life, you will do some bad things, but a lot of great things too. You will find that some people won't like anything you do, no matter how great it might be. You might think you've done the best thing in the world or took the only course of action there was to take, and there will still be those who'll hate you for it. You just can't be everyone's cup of tea."

I think of Bart Kingsley, with his puffy face, far-set eyes, and piggish nose, and how my very presence seemed to offend him. His words replay in my mind: *Seriously, did your great grandma name you or something? Was she, like, married to a cowboy?*

*Nice shoes. Did you get them at the church yard sale?*

"Were you pleased with yourself back then?" I ask, shaking away all thought of Bart. "For fighting in 'Nam?"

Grandpa casts a weary glance off the side of the porch. "No, I wasn't. A bunch of us thought we'd be heroes if we survived. But after seeing so much, we felt guilty for living. A lot of wives lost great husbands, and children lost great fathers. It just wasn't fair."

"Well," I say, "if you had died, then I wouldn't have a grandpa. I wouldn't even be here! Grandma wouldn't have anyone else to fuss to, either."

He chuckles. "You're right. Things would sure be different." Winking, he adds, "Wonder who Ella would've found to nag instead."

From the other side of the porch, Sandy's dog collar jingles. A moment later, she trots over to us and plops down on her back, begging for a belly rub.

Grandpa strokes her with his boot. "Spoiled rotten," he says, a slight smile on his lips.

The dog's eyes close, her pink tongue hanging out the side of her mouth, like it's the best feeling in the world. If only life could be as simple for humans as it is for dogs.

Grandpa looks down at her, but his gaze is unfocused, his head cocked to the side. I'd daresay he's lost in the past, back in those thick Vietnam jungles. I look away before he can notice me staring. There's something I want to tell him, but I don't know if I can; something I've thought about for a long time, just never put into words.

Grandpa speaks before I can say anything. "Ever since 'Nam, I've tried to make something of myself, put a little good in the world. Don't know how well I've succeeded, really. Thankfully, I met Ella, and she helped me not to feel so alone, so angry. Then you came into my life and changed it for the better." He taps his boots together. "Alright. Enough talking. It's time for breakfast."

"Grandpa?"

"Hmmm?"

*Just tell him,* I think. *Tell him how you feel.*

A hard lump forms in my throat, and it takes me a minute before I can get my words out. "For some, what you did in 'Nam might not mean anything. But to me, it means the world."

Grandpa turns away for a moment, and when he turns back, his eyes are a little glossier. "Well then," he says. "Maybe I have done something right."

# *16*
# GRANDMA'S GARDEN

RHETT AND I spend our first Saturday together as two bored boys with nothing to do. We look for box turtles in the creek, chase a half-tame rabbit around the yard, explore Grandpa's tool shed while he's out in the fields, build a fort at the edge of the woods, and shoot my BB gun at tin cans behind the barn. We only break twice—once for lunch and another for watermelon—and then we're off again. By supper, I'm sunburned, mosquito-bit, and drained of all energy. But not Rhett—I'm convinced he could run to Ms. Jean's front porch and back fifty times and still not be tired.

After a hearty portion of chicken and dumplings for supper that makes me full as a tick, we all gather in the living room to watch *The Lone Ranger*. Well, almost all of us.

"Where's Grandma?" I ask, raising my voice to be heard over the loud cracks from the Lone Ranger's pistol.

"That was a close one, wasn't it, Rhett?" says Grandpa from his recliner.

"Hi-yo, Silver! Away!" Rhett cheers, tipping his cowboy hat.

"Grandpa? Did you hear me?"

"Huh?" Grandpa grabs the remote and turns down the volume from thirty-eight to thirteen. "Clint, you sayin' somethin' over there?"

"Where's Grandma?" I ask again.

"Shoot if I know! She ain't botherin' me, so I'm not too worried about it." He turns the volume back up.

"Guess I'll find her myself," I mumble.

I find her outside, in the garden. She holds a rake in her hands, scraping away at the dirt. Green weeds cling between the rake's finger-like prongs. "Thought I'd find you out here."

Grandma straightens at the sound of my voice, propping the rake against her hip. "Is it just you?" she says, turning to face me. "Where's Rhett?"

"Inside with Grandpa, watching westerns."

Grandma rolls her eyes. "No surprise there. I know those westerns aren't your favorite. I'm not too fond of 'em myself. You've seen one, you've seen 'em all." She starts scraping away at the dirt again.

It's nearly nightfall, the vast evening sky as resplendent and intricate as that quilt hanging from the wooden knob on the side of Grandma's dresser. This sky is like the work of a seamstress, sown tangerine-orange, raspberry-pink, and dappled with cream-white clouds for an extra touch, the finished product so lush and vibrant that I could gape at it for hours.

Besides the scraping of Grandma's rake, the only sounds are the whine of mosquitoes and the chorus of cicadas out in the fields. "What are you doing out here, Grandma? It'll be dark soon."

"Just needed to get my mind off things, I reckon. Henry had the news on, which didn't help. In fact, it only raised my blood pressure. Reporters on there arguing about stuff that doesn't matter, like if Dolly Parton wears a wig or how many young'uns Nick Cannon has. Give me a break." Her voice rises, and she rakes faster with short, quick strokes. "Talk about something important, like where I can get a good senior discount or where I can find that red lipstick Taylor Swift uses. I need me some."

"Grandma, are you okay?"

She stops raking and looks at me sort of funny over her shoulder. "Well, I've been better."

"What's the matter?"

"There's just a lot going on right now."

"Like what? Can you tell me?"

Grandma doesn't answer, staring past the rows of peas, squash, field corn, and the rickety garden gate. She takes a deep breath.

"Is this about Rhett?" I ask.

His name seems to snap her from her daze. "Most of it." She sighs, wiping the sweat off her forehead. I notice she's not wearing her bandanna like usual; she must be distracted.

"When your grandpa and I took you in," she says,

talking real soft, "we didn't ever dream of Rhett coming to live with us. We're old, Clint. We retired to settle down, not raise another young'un. Besides, things have changed. It's not like when we came up. Just look at your homework. I feel like this is too big of a responsibility, and I don't want to let you boys down."

"You're not letting us down. And believe me, you're not old. You should see some of my teachers."

Grandma shakes her head. "Son, I'm sixty-eight. Your grandpa's seventy. Believe me, we're old. Raising two children is expensive. The court system's also all in sorts with Rhett right now."

"What does that mean?"

"It's too complicated for me to try and explain to an eleven-year-old."

"Well, will Rhett be able to stay here?"

Grandma sighs again, looking down at the ground. "We don't know. Me and your grandpa had this talk the other night. If we make this commitment, we have to have enough energy and resources to make it work. We can't just give him back after a few months."

"Oh. I see."

"I know this has been a difficult adjustment for you, but it's been difficult for me too. There ain't anything simple about raising a child. It's messy and complicated and painful and wonderful all at once. But it ain't simple. In ten years, Rhett will be seventeen. We don't even know if we'll be here in ten years! We could be in the nursing home, and if that's the case, who's going to take care of him?"

"Don't worry, Grandma. I can do it."

She stares at me for a moment, her bottom lip trembling. "That's mighty brave of you, Clint, but you can't let that stop you from living your dreams."

"I know," I say, "but that's what brothers have to do. We take care of each other."

Grandma turns away and makes a sniffling sound. When she turns back—her eyes a little shinier—she nods and offers a weak smile. "That's right."

She takes another deep breath, but this time, her body shudders a little. Seeing Grandma this stressed about raising Rhett makes me wonder.

"Why did you decide to let Rhett come live with us?"

"Because," she says, propping the rake back against her hip, "I believe everyone deserves a chance."

"Everyone?"

*Even cruel people, like Bart Kingsley?* I think.

"Yes, everyone," Grandma says. "Because most people in bad situations don't have a chance. Most of them don't have anyone to care for them or raise them up right. Take this garden for instance: if we let the weeds take over, and didn't fertilize or water the plants, the garden would waste away. In fact, that's one of the reasons I'm out here now. The weeds grow fast, and in about a month, they'll choke out everything good. It's like life. As your grandma, I've got to do my part while you boys are young, so you can become something.

"I don't know if I've told you this"—Grandma swats at a mosquito buzzing around her face—"but when I was a young'un, my parents left me."

"They left you?"

"Yep," Grandma says. "But you know something

good that comes out of a bad situation? It's that the Lord puts great people in your path, and I went to live with my granny, a spunky half-Indian woman."

"What was she like?"

"Well, she was real short for one. She had long brown hair that she kept pulled back in a bun, and she always wore an apron tied around her waist. The apron had two pockets. She kept money in one pocket and her snuff box in the other." Grandma smiles, staring off into the distance again like she's caught in a memory. "My granny cooked on a wood stove until the day she died. She never owned an electric one. She canned her own vegetables in glass jars and heated the wash pot over open flame.

"She had a temper, let me tell you. And when she got mad, her blue eyes would spark fire. Her mouth would get the upper hand too, if you know what I mean." Grandma chuckles. "She couldn't stand bad weather. Every time lightning flashed, she covered all the windows and mirrors with quilts. One time," she says, smiling even bigger, "a light bulb busted in the house during a gully washer, and she hollered, *'Lord help!'* Let me tell you: we thought she had gone to glory."

"That's funny," I say, chuckling. I close my eyes and try to picture her, the way she looked, the way she dressed. I imagine her granny wore a bandanna tied around her head, too. I bet she smelled like baby powder and vanilla, just like Grandma. "Sounds like I would've really liked her."

"You would've," she says, "and she would've loved you. That's the thing—even though I wasn't her young'un, she loved me. She raised me on sweet tea and snap peas, and for that, I'll forever be grateful. Now, I'm trying to do the same for you, Clint. And Rhett. You boys deserve every bit of love and care, just the same as any young'un."

"Thank you," I tell her.

"No, thank you, son. Without you, life just wouldn't be the same."

# 17

# THE CHURCH CHICKEN

IT'S SUNDAY—MY GRANDPARENT'S favorite day of the week. To them, Sundays are good for three things: church, rest, and fried chicken from Piggly Wiggly.

I don't mind church too much. Sure, it can be long sometimes—especially when Pastor Tom preaches on the book of Revelation—but other than school and the grocery store, church is one of my only opportunities to get away from the farm.

Magnolia Springs is a white cinderblock community church, and real tricky to find. The building lies at the end of a four-mile dirt road, nestled up against some large oak trees and a sprawling cemetery. When the wind blows just right, tree branches scrape against the church's tin roof, sounding like a beast trying to claw its way inside. Whenever that happens, the old people either start adjusting their hearing aids or praying, and Pastor Tom starts sweating and preaching a little faster.

A few cars, mostly older-model sedans, are already parked outside the church when we arrive. I recognize all the cars and all the people; in my entire five years of living with Grandma and Grandpa, I haven't missed one Sunday here.

Grandpa parks and we walk up the ramp leading to the glass doors.

Rhett—who pouted all morning because Grandma wouldn't let him wear his cowboy hat to church—steps in front of me, clearly unaware of what's in store for him inside Magnolia Springs.

"If you don't want your cheeks pinched," I tell Rhett, "then stay close."

He might only be seven, but with one look inside the small sanctuary, he understands what I mean. We're the only children here, probably the youngest people to walk through these doors in decades.

Inside, making their way around on canes and aluminum walkers, are the current oldest members of Magnolia Springs Church: Linda-Sue, who always smells like baby powder and has a pet chicken named Pearl that rides to church with her; Francis, whose lisp makes the hymn "Blessed Assurance" sound like a foreign language; David, who lost his left hand in a hay baler;

Myrtle, who sort of looks like a vulture, with a hunched-over stance, a long, hooked nose, beady eyes, and a nearly bald head save for a few white, wispy tufts of hair; Josephine, who has only one good eye since the other is made of glass (the last time she bent over to pick up a nickel during church, her glass eye fell out and rolled down front between two pews); and Curtis, who I'm fairly certain hasn't showered in years. He smells like a rotten potato, probably because he worked at the butcher pen for so long that the smell practically seeped into his skin. Wherever he goes, there's at least two or three flies buzzing around him.

"Who's this fine-looking feller you've got with you?" Myrtle squawks, hobbling over to us on her silver cane. She holds up a hand, her arthritic fingers already moving back and forth like bird claws.

I practically snatch Rhett behind me before she can pinch his cheeks. "This is Rhett. He's living with us right now."

Myrtle nods and peeks behind my back. "Young man, do you like peach cobbler?" she asks Rhett.

Nodding, Rhett stares up at the woman with wide eyes. If I had to guess, Myrtle is probably the oldest woman he's ever seen. Only by the grace of God does Myrtle suddenly notice Grandma coming down the aisle. The two strike up a conversation while Rhett and I go find ourselves a seat.

The sanctuary smells like mothballs and old carnations, and the only light comes in through orange stained-glass windows. Ten pews run along either side of the center aisle, which leads to a large, white altar where Pastor Tom always keeps his Bible.

The service starts with prayer. After that, it's time to sing. Rhett and I share a red leather-bound hymnal, one so old the spine creaks every time you turn a page. I'm convinced one hard breath would turn the pages loose. I notice David farther down the row prop the book on his nub and flip the yellow pages with his only good hand. Not that a hymnal does any good; the women get half of the words wrong and repeat the first verse three times.

Myrtle sings the loudest, though I really shouldn't call it singing; honestly, it's more like screeching. Francis tries her best, but her lisp makes her sound like she's singing two notes behind everyone else. Curtis, attempting to sing bass, makes low, throaty noises oddly similar to a bullfrog. All the while, Linda-Sue confidently taps away at the piano, even if she gets most of the notes wrong in the process. I can't stop staring at her foot, stomping the piano pedals like a clutch on a car.

The entire twenty-minute worship service is a chaotic circus of noise. At one point, Rhett even puts his hands over his ears. Not that I blame him; it sounds worse than the strings of a badly tuned violin.

Not a second too soon, Pastor Tom, a pudgy, gray-haired man who I'd guess is in his early seventies, starts preaching. He has a deep, baritone voice like Johnny Cash that makes me want to fall asleep. "Every day you are at war with the devil," says Pastor Tom.

"Amen!" Myrtle squawks from the front pew.

"Amen, brother!" Curtis croaks.

Pastor Tom goes on. "One day Jesus is going to appear in the Eastern sky, and we know how that ends. He wins!"

"Amen!" Grandma says from beside me, making me jump.

"Amen, pastor!" Myrtle chimes in again. "Praise the Lord!"

To me, the church people are like a bunch of chickens—when one clucks, another one starts up, until eventually they're all clucking.

"He's coming soon, friends!" Pastor Tom shouts. "Can I get an amen?"

Instead, Myrtle lets loose a bloodcurdling scream, making the hairs on the back of my neck stand on end. Rhett jumps to a standing position, startled.

Heads turn to look at Myrtle.

She screams for a second time, raising her legs and pointing down at the floor. "Pastor," she yells, "there's a chicken loose in here!"

"My Pearly!" says Linda-Sue. "I bet she slipped out my car window."

There's a flap of wings as Pearl jumps onto the pew with Myrtle. The brown chicken looks at the woman with one beady eye.

"Somebody get that chicken out of here," Pastor Tom huffs. "This is a house of God! No chickens allowed."

"Pastor?" a panicked voice says.

Heads turn to look, this time toward the back of the church.

The voice belongs to Josephine, who's currently holding a hand over her face. "Pastor," she says again, "I turned my head too fast and my eye popped out. Can one of y'all help me find it?"

"Lord Almighty," says Pastor Tom, shaking his head.

"Bless her heart," Grandma whispers.

Rhett points toward the center aisle. "There it goes!" he says.

Holding my breath, I turn to look.

Sure enough, Josephine's glass eye rolls down the aisle like a marble, headed straight for the altar.

Pearl clucks, louder this time, flapping her wings as she hops over a screaming Myrtle. Pearl lands in the center aisle, gaze trained on the rolling glass eye.

Francis stands and yells, "Pastah, hep her!"

Grandpa says, "Stop that chicken!"

Myrtle screeches, "Lord, be with us!"

Within seconds, the entire congregation is hollering and pointing. That's why I don't notice Rhett slip past me until it's too late. He darts into the aisle, shooting across the floor, chasing Josephine's eye.

Pearl gets to it first, poking at the eye with her beak. In her scuffle, she knocks it back toward Rhett, who lunges and snatches the eye up. "Got it!" he says with a big grin, holding the eye between his thumb and forefinger.

"Watch out!" Myrtle shrieks, pointing a long, trembling finger.

Rhett's smile falls from his face when he notices Pearl racing toward him.

At that moment, Pastor Tom tugs off his coat, steps forward, and throws it over Pearl. Then, he bends over, picks up the coat with the chicken and walks out the back door, Pearl squawking and flapping all the while.

Hot on the pastor's heels, Linda-Sue cries, "Pearl, don't let him hurt you!" She slips out the door behind the pastor and her rebellious chicken.

The moment they're gone, the congregation begins clapping.

"Dat waz a sight," Francis says behind me.

"Rhett, give Ms. Josephine her eye back," says Grandpa.

"Okay." Rhett grins wider and drops the eye in Josephine's outstretched palm.

"Thank you, son." Josephine wipes it on her shirt and places it on the tip of her tongue for a moment. Then, with a small pop, she inserts the eye back into her socket. "There. All better." She looks around at the congregation with a smile.

I turn to Rhett and wink. "Welcome to Magnolia Springs Church," I whisper.

# *18*
## THERESA, THE TWIDDLER

RIGHT AFTER CHURCH, my great Aunt Theresa comes to visit. She drives one of those long white Cadillacs which is so old that I can hear the muffler long before I spot the car. Whenever it sounds like a log truck is tearing down our drive, nine times out of ten it's my great Aunt Theresa.

Out of all of Grandpa's sisters, she is the only one I can remember. Not because she always stores a pinch of snuff between her cheek and gum and not because a puff of brown dust escapes her mouth every time she speaks. It's because my great Aunt Theresa is a twiddler. She's constantly twiddling with something—a strand of hair, her nails, an earlobe, a sock, the bottom of her shoe. But in the past five years, she's developed a new twiddling habit—trailing her fingers up and down pillowcase fabric. In fact, she stores pillowcases everywhere, like in the trunk of her car or in the oversized purse always swinging from her hip. Where most people can't go five minutes without their phone, Aunt Theresa can't go five minutes without her pillowcase.

We're on the porch sitting around a picnic table, Grandma cutting into a large watermelon to split among the four of us, when we hear her coming. The exhaust pipes on Aunt Theresa's car pump out a steady rhythm, kind of like a woodpecker hammering on a hollow tree. As she comes to a screeching halt in the yard, the brakes squeal.

Grandma cuts the watermelon faster. "Goodness gracious," she mumbles, slicing a kitchen knife down the rind. The melon falls in two halves with a wet smack. "Quick, boys. I hear the old witch riding in on her broom. Hurry up and eat before she gets any closer."

"Why?" asks Rhett, darting glances between Aunt Theresa's Cadillac and Grandma hunched over the picnic table. "Can she not have any?"

"Nope. She can get her own melon. I bought three of these myself. Paid six dollars each for 'em. So no, she can't have any."

Grandpa rolls his eyes. "Oh, Ella. Let it go." He looks at Rhett. "Of course she can have some. She's family."

Grandma saws a corner of the melon so hard that her knife cuts into the wood table; she looks like she's about to fly off the handle. "Theresa's always taking something from me. A pie, a cake, fried chicken, or my pillowcases. And she never brings anything back to make up for it."

"Your pillowcases?" Rhett asks.

"Yep. She's clearly only got one oar in the water. It must run in the family."

Grandpa rolls his eyes again. At this point, I'm surprised they haven't gotten stuck in the back of his head. "Hey, quit being ugly. These boys don't need to hear any of your nonsense right now. Doesn't matter if she's crazier than a sprayed roach, she's my sister, and I'm lucky to have her. Now get to cutting, and leave some for our guest."

Grandma gets real quiet after that. I notice that when Aunt Theresa finally steps out of her car and waves to us, Grandma turns her back, never breaking stare from the melon that she's sawed into about fifty pieces.

"Hello, stranger," Grandpa says to Aunt Theresa. "Long time no see."

"I hope I'm not interruptin'," she says back, hobbling up the porch steps. She's wearing high-waist jeans that ride almost up to her bra, and a Mickey-Mouse T-shirt that looks like it's been through the wash a few too many times—the sleeves sag, the collar is stretched a little too low, and Mickey's milk-white hue has turned a couple shades too dark. Her gray hair is pulled back into a sloppy bun—several strands bounce around her face as she steps closer to the picnic table—and when she smiles, I notice red lipstick smeared across her snuff-stained teeth.

In her hands is a long white pillowcase. As she talks, her fingers travel up and down it in scissoring motions. "Figured y'all could use some company," she says, a puff of brown dust escaping her mouth.

"Shoot," says Grandpa, "you must've known I needed a break from Ella."

Theresa tosses her head back and cackles.

"Alright now," Grandma mumbles.

As Aunt Theresa plops down in a chair beside Grandpa, her beady eyes settle on Rhett. "And who is this little feller?"

"I'm Rhett," he says, a mischievous glint in his eye.

"This here is one of Ella's cousins," Grandpa says. "He's going to be staying with us for a while."

"Well, ain't he cute." Aunt Theresa looks at Rhett and winks.

Rhett smiles, showing all of his teeth. He points to the center of the table. "Want some watermelon? Grandma saved you a piece."

Across the table, I notice Grandma's cheeks turn as red as the fruit on her plate. I bite into my piece of watermelon to keep from chuckling, the sweet, crisp flavor filling my mouth with a cold explosion.

"Why, sure," Aunt Theresa says, her thumb and forefinger rubbing together as she reaches for a slice. "Ain't that thoughtful."

"We got plenty," Rhett says in between bites of watermelon. Red juice covers his lips and trickles down his chin. "In fact, Grandma's got two more in the kitchen, and she'd probably let you take one home. Isn't that right, Grandma?"

Grandma blinks once, twice, before forcing a smile. I can tell it's fake because her eyes look a little too pinched together, almost like she's squinting. It's also the first time she's looked at Aunt Theresa since she arrived. "Tell us," Grandma says, changing the subject, "how have you been?"

The pillowcase now laying across her lap, Theresa nibbles the piece of watermelon like an ear of corn before coming up for breath. I try not to stare, but I can't help it. "Well," she says, wiping her mouth with the back of her hand, "I've been doin' alright, 'cept for my gallbladder."

"Oh. Are they going to cut your gallbladder out?" asks Grandma.

"No, the doctors just told me to cut out all my grease. But I got to have my fried chicken, so they'll just have to deal with it."

"Yeah. You and Henry both," says Grandma.

No one says anything for a few moments, the only sound the slurping and chewing of watermelon. There's a quiver in my stomach due to the awkward silence, and the feeling worsens when Grandma looks over at Aunt Theresa and wrinkles her nose. I look away, hoping Aunt Theresa didn't notice.

Grandpa picks up the saltshaker from the table. "This is how it's done, boys," he says, raining salt onto his piece of watermelon.

Rhett's face scrunches up like he's tasted something foul. "Ewww, Grandpa. That's gross!"

"Can't knock it 'til you've tried it, son." After taking a big bite and wiping his sticky hands on his navy-blue work shirt, Grandpa leans back and adds, "Ain't as good as sweet tea and snap peas, but it'll do."

## 19
## THE MISPLACED PILLOWCASE

WE SIT ON the porch for what seems like hours. While the adults talk, Rhett and I stuff our faces with watermelon, having a competition to see who can spit the seeds the farthest.

Our game doesn't last very long before Grandma gives us the eye, and we both quit.

Thankfully, Sandy comes trotting over from beneath the porch swing to keep us occupied. I scratch behind her rusty-red ears while Rhett sneaks her a piece of watermelon.

While her fingers travel up and down her pillowcase, Aunt Theresa clears her throat and says, "Y'all know my birthday's comin' up."

Grandpa nods. "Yep. You'll be seventy-five."

"No, seventy-four."

"You can tell that lie if you want to," Grandpa says, "but Daddy wrote it in the family Bible the hour you were born."

"Well, he was drunk most of the time. I wouldn't believe half of what he wrote in that thing."

"He might've been drunk, but he could still write. I remember it, too. You were born in the back bedroom, and I sat on that cedar chest with Daddy, waiting for you to come."

"The spawn of the devil," Grandma mumbles. She must think no one can hear her.

Rhett stops feeding Sandy watermelon long enough to ask, "What was that, Grandma?"

"Didn't I tell you to go wash your hands?" she asks him.

"I did," Rhett says.

She glares at him for a second.

"Why lie about your age anyway?" Grandpa asks, clasping his hands behind his head. "Don't tell me you're still mad that they held you back in the fourth grade."

"Fourth and fifth grade, prob'ly," Grandma mutters.

Aunt Theresa looks at Grandma across the table. "Ella, you sayin' somethin' over there?"

But Grandpa doesn't wait for Grandma to speak. "Oh, you just didn't want to tell everybody at high school graduation that you were twenty years old." He rolls his eyes. "It didn't stop you when you started dating at fourteen, did it?"

"Fourteen?" I pipe up. "You started dating at fourteen?"

"I did not!" Theresa squeals. Clearly Grandpa's

struck a nerve; her fingers move so fast along the pillowcase I'm afraid she's going to tear a hole in it. "Your grandpa just likes to make things up."

"Well, Grandma says I'm not allowed to date until I'm seventeen."

"That's right," Grandma replies.

Theresa says, "Oh, come on, Ella. You and Henry started datin' a lot sooner than seventeen."

I stop petting Sandy. So does Rhett. "You did?" I ask her.

Grandpa rises from his chair. "I think it's time to head inside. I could use some tea. Mouth's getting dry."

"And I'm getting a headache," Grandma grumbles.

"Wait a minute." Aunt Theresa stops twiddling and looks down at her lap. "Where'd my pillowcase go?"

"Whadd'ya mean where'd your pillowcase go?" Grandpa says. "It's right there in your hands."

"No, Henry, I don't mean this one. My *other* pillowcase. I had it right here…right in my lap."

"What the heck you need two for?"

"Can you hush and help me look for it?" Aunt Theresa bends down to peek under her chair. "It's around here somewhere."

"Well, it didn't just grow legs and walk off," Grandma says. "Whadd'ya reckon you did with it?"

"Who knows! Guess I'm losin' my dadgum mind."

"Come on, boys. Help us look," says Grandpa.

The longer it takes to find Aunt Theresa's pillowcase, the crazier she seems to get. Her eyes widen, her breathing increases to a huffing sound, and her upper body starts rocking back and forth in her chair. I might not know any better, but I think she's having a panic attack.

"Are you alright?" I ask her.

"Shut up and help me find it!" she huffs.

Gasping, Rhett says, "Aunt Theresa just said a bad word!"

"What? I did not!"

Grandma hits her wedding ring against her tea glass. "Can everybody hush? My head's pounding."

Grandpa looks between me, Rhett, and Grandma. "This ain't funny. Whoever took it, hand it over."

No one says anything.

Grandpa narrows his eyes and lowers his voice. "Rhett, are you behind this? If so, give my sister her pillowcase back."

Rhett throws up his hands and says, "It wasn't me! I've been petting the dog!"

"I don't see any dog," says Grandpa.

"She was just here," I say, "sitting right under the table."

"Sandy!" Grandpa calls, cupping both hands over his mouth. "Oh, Sandy! C'mere, girl."

"Grandma, can't you just give her another pillowcase?" asks Rhett.

Grandma doesn't answer; she's too busy staring at Aunt Theresa.

Tears form in the woman's eyes, lips quivering, as she twirls a strand of gray hair between her fingers. "You don't understand," she sniffles, rocking back and forth, "that pillowcase belonged to my momma. It's the only one I have left from her. And now...now it's *gone*."

Theresa starts sobbing.

I bite my lip and close my eyes. *God, please help us find my aunt's pillowcase,* I think. *I'm worried about her. I don't want her to be upset.*

I open my eyes. To my surprise, Grandma's standing beside Theresa, rubbing her back. "It's okay. We'll find it," she whispers. "Now quit that crying."

That's when I hear a growling noise coming from the end of the porch—the same noise Sandy makes when she's biting her fur to rid herself of fleas. I turn toward the sound.

Sure enough, it's Sandy—white strips and shreds lie at her feet, a hundred of them it seems.

Grandpa sucks in a breath.

Grandma mutters, "Bless it be."

Rhett and I gasp.

Aunt Theresa sobs louder.

All the while, Sandy looks at us and smiles, a white piece of pillowcase fabric hanging from the side of her mouth.

# 20
# BUTTERBEANS & MS. JEAN

BART ISN'T AT school the next day, so I don't have to worry too much. At this point, I don't know where we stand. Is he mad at me? Is he planning to get back at me? Or is he done trying altogether?

At lunch, I sit by myself. Eat in silence. Read my book while the others talk and laugh and occasionally beat their fists against the lunchroom tables. I can't tell if they genuinely like school, or if they're just pretending. Maybe they're all really good actors, unlike me. Their conversations are strange, filled with language I don't understand. They all sound the same, too, as if they're following a script no one bothered to share with me. Until middle school, I never knew people could say so much without saying much of anything at all.

I wish Aaliyah was here. Or Rhett. Or Grandma and Grandpa.

I wish making friends was as easy as the books and movies make it seem.

I wish I felt more like a person, not like some ghost seeing everyone, hearing everything, without anyone noticing it.

I wish kindness would get me farther than sitting alone, my throat thick with sadness.

Besides Aaliyah, everyone I talk to at this place stares at me like I'm some bug-eyed creature, so I keep my mouth shut as much as possible. Confide in books because they don't judge.

I've become the best at being invisible, sticking to the role I was assigned.

Maybe I'm a decent actor after all.

That afternoon, Rhett comes home from school with an announcement.

"I'm going to plant Ms. Jean a garden," he says.

"A garden?" Grandma arches a brow. "Well, that's mighty thoughtful of you. But why Ms. Jean?"

"Because," Rhett says, pulling a small bag out of the front of his backpack, "my teacher gave me these butter-bean seeds to take home, but we already have a garden. Ms. Jean doesn't."

I'm sure if Rhett knew Ms. Jean, he wouldn't bother—the woman is as curious as a calf staring at a new gate. She's always watering grass she doesn't have or watching us through binoculars from her front porch. One day, when the police came by after Grandma accidentally dialed 911, Ms. Jean brought us a pound cake, most likely to find out why the cops were in our yard. I'd cracked the door and took the cake without explanation, just to leave her wondering.

Grandma sighs. "Alright. Just don't invite her over here."

"I'll help him, Grandma," I say. "Ms. Jean won't interrogate him if I'm there."

Grandma shakes her head and mumbles, "Good luck," before heading outside to work in the garden.

We don't even have to ring Ms. Jean's doorbell. She's on the front porch the instant we step into her yard.

"Hello, gentlemen," she calls out to us, both hands on her round hips, and a sneaky smile plastered across her face. "What brings you to my place?"

"I'm going to plant you a garden!" Rhett says, holding up his bag of butterbean seeds.

Short, plump, gray-haired Ms. Jean puts a fleshy hand to her heart. "That is *too* sweet," she says with a little high-pitched giggle. "How *considerate*." Something flashes behind her eyes and her upper lip twitches. "Now, what's your name, dear?" Her gaze is focused on Rhett. "Are you kin to Henry and Ella?"

"This is Rhett," I say. "He's my little brother."

Ms. Jean lets out a little gasp. "Your brother...well, I didn't know you had a—"

"Guess there's a lot you don't know about us, Ms. Jean." Her smile disappears. She blinks at me several times.

I look away, forcing a grin. "Now, where would you like for us to put your garden?"

Ms. Jean's smile returns. "Oh, yes…that's right, *the garden*." She giggles again. "Anywhere here around the porch would be nice."

"Alright. We can do that," I tell her.

For the next half hour, we dig Ms. Jean up a garden using one of her garden hoes. Then, with a rake, we rid the weeds from the dirt, and form small rows for the butterbeans. I use a stick to punch a hole for the seeds, but Rhett just uses his index finger.

At one point, Ms. Jean disappears into her house. No less than five minutes later, she's on the porch again, a coffee cup in hand, watching us. Once, I notice her staring at me with a nasty snarl, but when I meet her gaze, the snarl vanishes behind the rim of her coffee cup.

Eventually, I decide Rhett can finish up. I have a lot of homework to catch up on and Rhett seems to have it under control. Before I go, I lean down and whisper in his ear. "If she bothers you, just say you need to run home and get something. You don't have to come back." I sneak a quick glance at her over my shoulder. She's sitting on the top porch step, leafing through the pages of a *Southern Homes and Gardens* magazine. Every couple moments, she looks over the top of her book at us.

"Don't worry, Clint. I've got this," Rhett says.

I leave without another word.

The next morning, during the middle of breakfast, someone pounds on the front door.

Rhett and I race to open it, but he gets there first.

"Oh, hello, Ms. Jean," says Rhett. "Do you like your garden?"

The voice that replies sounds nothing like our peppy-voiced neighbor. "No, I don't like my garden! In fact, I *hate* it! My yard is ruined!"

When I join Rhett at the door and look out onto the porch, my mouth drops open. It's Ms. Jean, alright—water drips from the ends of her gray hair, her hands are black from what I assume to be dirt, and her blue jeans are splattered with mud all the way up to her knees.

"What happened, Ms. Jean?" asks Rhett.

Biting back a laugh, I say, "Yeah, what...what happened?"

Ms. Jean's lips twist into a snarl. She stabs a finger in Rhett's face. "This little *twit*! That's what happened! He left the hose on *all night* and flooded my yard! *Flooded* it, I tell you!

"To make matters worse, some raccoons dug up that place looking for those seeds. I checked, and they're all *gone*! All *gone*, I tell you!"

Grandma's by my side in an instant. She must've heard Ms. Jean all the way from the dining room. "Rhett did *what*?" she asks, looking our neighbor up and down. She turns to face him. "Rhett, is this true?"

Cheeks as red as the side of a fire truck, Rhett looks down and says, "Yes, Grandma. I was trying to water the garden so the seeds would grow. I'm sorry."

"Don't tell me sorry. Tell Ms. Jean."

Still looking down at his feet, Rhett says, "I'm sorry, Ms. Jean."

"Like you mean it," Grandma adds.

Rhett raises his voice. "I'm sorry, Ms.—"

"Save it!" snaps our neighbor. "I don't want to hear your useless apology. I want you to *fix* it!"

Grandma stiffens like a board. "Boys, how about y'all go get ready for school?"

"But I've already—"

"Get ready for school," she repeats, narrowing her eyes at Rhett.

"Yes ma'am," he says.

"And Ms. Jean," Grandma says, turning back to our soaking-wet, teeth-chattering neighbor, "we'll talk about this later. Have a good—"

"You listen to me, Ella! If you don't get a handle of this hooligan boy," says Ms. Jean, cutting her cold eyes over to Rhett, "I'll put in a word with Child Services. Maybe sending this twit to live somewhere else will teach him a lesson. He needs discipline, not some grandma who can't even keep a close eye on him. If he steps foot in my yard again—"

Grandma shuts the door in Ms. Jean's face. Then she turns the deadbolt with a harsh click. "Boys," she says, turning to us, "don't go back over there without me or your grandpa, ya hear?"

"Yes ma'am," I say, my heart racing at Ms. Jean's comment. *I'll put in a word with Child Services.* She wouldn't really do that, would she?

"But Grandma!" says Rhett. "I had a reason to leave

the water on. My teacher told me the seeds would come up quicker if they were wet."

Grandma wags a finger back and forth in his face. "Don't fret it, son. That woman's trouble." She walks back into the dining room without another word.

When I'm sure she's far enough away not to hear, I lower my voice and ask, "It wasn't an accident, was it?"

Rhett doesn't say anything. He just smiles up at me.

"Did Ms. Jean say something to you after I left? Is that why you flooded her yard?"

"She wouldn't leave me alone," he says. "She kept asking me about my parents, who I was related to, all kinds of stuff. She hurt my feelings! It's none of her business."

"So you flooded her yard? Why didn't you just go home like I told you?"

Rhett shrugs. "She had it coming. She shouldn't bother us anymore. Besides, when I get to school, I'm going to tell my teacher that I planted a woman's garden. She said if we do something nice for someone she'll buy us our favorite candy bar."

I sigh and rub my forehead. "Rhett, you can't do that! That's not right."

"Yes, it is! I did exactly what she told me. Now I get a treat."

"But that's lying. That's a sin!"

"So is calling a little kid a twit," Rhett says, turning in the direction of the dining room. "She knows better! I'm only seven."

He sounds just like Grandma and Grandpa. It's only been a week—one that's felt like forever—but they've already rubbed off on him. I can't even be mad. He has a point.

"Still." I shake my head. "All this for a candy bar?"

Before I join them back at the dining room table to finish breakfast, I glance out the window beside the front door.

Ms. Jean's gone, but a trail of muddy footprints lead from our porch, down the steps, and beyond—all the way back to her flooded front yard.

I almost feel bad for her. Almost.

At the end of breakfast, while Rhett's gone to get his library book which he left in our room, I ask Grandma, "Do you think Ms. Jean was serious about calling Child Services? Do you think she'll get him sent away?"

Grandma swallows a bite of oatmeal. "I won't let her, hon. Don't you worry. She's just talking nonsense."

"But you said the other day that Rhett might not be able to stay here. That you might not have enough energy to make it work—"

"I know what I said, Clint. But you have to remember I was under a lot of stress. You know I talk out of my head when I'm stressed." Grandma must notice the doubtful look on my face. "Everything will be okay. Rhett's not going anywhere. I promise."

I look back down at my plate of eggs and bacon. I really want to trust her, but a small part of me worries that her promise might be difficult to keep.

# *21*
## THE TRUTH

On the bus later that morning, Aaliyah hands me an Airpod.

"What's this for?" I ask, looking up from Rhett's library book. Lately, I've been trying to help him read every spare moment. Besides, it keeps him occupied and gives him less opportunity to drive me insane.

"Remember when I said I'd let you listen to Aaliyah? Well, I meant it." She sticks an Airpod in her left ear. "Sit back and enjoy."

*If you say so,* I think.

I pop the Airpod in my ear and lean my head back against the seat.

The first song starts up; something about going back, back, forth, and forth. Then another about love going on and on and on.

After the third song, Aaliyah smiles at me from across the aisle. "So? What do you think?"

"It's different," I tell her, "but good. Real good. I've never heard anything quite like it. My grandparents only listen to country and gospel music. You know, Dolly Parton, Conway Twitty, Hank Williams, and Elvis. My grandma loves Elvis."

Aaliyah rolls her eyes. "Tell me about it. My granny loves him too. She said she cried the day he died."

"She cried? Why? She didn't know him, did she?"

Aaliyah shakes her head. "My granny? Please, she's never left the city limits! Of course she didn't know him."

"Well, why did she cry?"

"'Cause he meant a lot to her. Just like Aaliyah means a lot to me. I don't think you've got to really know people like Aaliyah and Elvis in order for them to feel real. You just got to listen to 'em sing. That's it. That way, you can hear everything they're going through at the same time. It's like magic."

"Who knew something as simple as listening could be magic."

Aaliyah looks down at her lap, her face turning serious. "Look, there's something I've been meaning to tell you."

I take out my Airpod. "What is it?"

Aaliyah tugs on her purple shirt. "Well, when I met you, I wasn't exactly telling the truth. I told you those boys in the back of the bus were being too loud and that's why I decided to move." Aaliyah shakes her head. "But that's not true. The truth is, nobody would let me sit with them. Nobody 'cept you."

My stomach flutters. "What do you mean they wouldn't let you sit with them? That's the dumbest thing I've ever heard!"

Aaliyah crosses her arms. "Maybe it's 'cause I'm different. I'm not popular or even that pretty. I guess that's why."

"That's not true," I say, shaking my head. "I think you're pretty." My cheeks burn once I realize what I've said. Then it gets quiet.

Aaliyah stares at the side of my face. "You really think so?" she finally says.

"Okay, this is getting awkward," Rhett mumbles beside me, looking up from his book.

I ignore him. "Yeah. I do think so. And who cares what anyone else thinks. Being popular is boring. It never lasts for long. I'd rather be myself than to have to change who I am to fit in. Like my grandpa says, 'You just can't be everyone's cup of tea.' There's nothing wrong with that."

"I'd rather be different, too." Aaliyah looks up at me and then looks back down at her lap. "My granny says being different makes a person special."

"That's right."

"It's kind of like those snap peas you told me about. How not many people give them a chance."

"That's right," I say again.

"You know, Clint…you're probably the nicest person I've met at this school."

"Really?" My cheeks grow warmer. I bet they're as red as Aunt Theresa's lipstick.

"Really," Aaliyah says. "Because you listen." She

chuckles. "Thanks for not telling me to go sit somewhere else."

"You're welcome. Thanks for sitting with me. You make the bus a lot less boring." My voice softens. "And I know what it feels like to be different. A lot of people make fun of how I talk. They say my accent makes me sound dumb."

"That's ridiculous. I love your accent! I couldn't imagine you without it. It's what makes you special, Clint."

Something warm and light spreads through my chest, and I can't keep from smiling. Aaliyah's words make me feel free. Content. If she had told me that a week ago, I might not have believed her like I do now.

Her words also make me realize something—everyone has at least one thing that makes them unique and special. Aunt Theresa and her pillowcases. Grandma and her bandanna. Grandpa and his boots. Rhett and his cowboy hat. Aaliyah and her infectious laugh. Me and my accent.

I pop the Airpod back in my ear. "Alright. What's next?"

Aaliyah slides a finger along the bottom of her phone screen. "Oh, I know. I've got a good one."

For the rest of the bus ride, we don't talk, we just listen. Rhett naps beside me, even slumps against my side at one point, a thin line of drool trickling from the corner of his mouth. I don't even bother telling him to move. I just let him sleep. Aaliyah mouths the lyrics to herself, bobbing her head in time with the music. Every now and then, she looks across the aisle at me and smiles. She probably thinks I don't notice, but I do.

After a few minutes, I lean back and close my eyes. I think about what my life was like before Aaliyah and Rhett. Then I shake the thought away, because I really don't want to remember.

At school, Bart doesn't talk to me. He doesn't kick the back of my chair in seventh period or toss paper airplanes at my back or whisper insults. It's as if he's done trying, which doesn't make sense. I would've thought that Rhett kicking Bart on the bus would have led to something bad, something worse. But Bart keeps his distance, acting like he's never spoken to me before.

While I'm glad Bart's seemed to learn his lesson, I'm surprised that he's treating me with silence. I wonder who he's moved on to torment now that I'm out of the picture. Does he talk to anyone? Does he have friends? I'm surprised that I care after all he's done to me. But Bart Kingsley is somewhat of a mystery. Why does he act so rude? Is it because he's lonesome, too? Like me?

After the bell rings, Bart is one of the first to leave the room. I follow him into the hall. As I try to catch up, I'm reminded of how much has changed between us. Now I'm the one following him, trying to get *his* attention.

I've almost caught up when Bart turns on his heel and faces me. "Stop following me, Cowgirl."

"I just wanted to say sorry. You know, for what Rhett did. I tried to stop him. I didn't want you to get hurt."

Bart presses his lips together until they turn white.

"I'm sorry," I say again. "Really."

"Sure you are."

"Please don't be mad at me—"

"Not everything's about you, Cowgirl." Bart turns away.

I stare after him for a moment, unsure of how to respond. As the hall fills with students, I make up my mind and follow him, quickening my step. "Can't we just drop this?" Bart shoves his way out the door at the end of the hall. Just before it shuts in my face, I push it open, only a couple steps behind him. "Can't we just talk without fighting? What's the point?" Bart doesn't turn around, doesn't even acknowledge me. Without thinking, I reach out and touch his shoulder. "Bart—"

"*Don't* touch me," he says, whipping around. "Don't talk to me. Just leave me alone. *Please.* I just want to be left alone."

When he turns away this time, I don't try and stop him. I just stand there, watching him go, wondering if, instead of helping things, I somehow made everything worse.

## 22

## SOMETHING MISSING

THAT AFTERNOON, AS Rhett and I finish up our homework and Grandma prepares supper, I notice something missing, kind of like when you walk outside and don't see the moon in the night sky and start to wonder why.

"Where's Grandpa?" I ask.

"I don't know," says Grandma, wiping both hands on her apron. "Now that you've mentioned it, I haven't seen him in a while."

"Want me to go look for him? He's usually inside watching westerns by now."

"I'll go get him," Rhett says, standing from his chair.

"I'll go with you."

We're almost at the front door when Grandma calls out, "Now that I think about it, he did tell me he was going across the creek to put up that deer stand. Check there first."

So that's what we do, crossing the front yard to a footbridge that leads over the tea-colored creek and into the woods. The whole walk only takes a minute, two minutes at most. Ahead of us come the high-pitched yips of a dog. *Sandy,* I think.

The barks grow louder with every step. Thirty feet away, I spot her rusty-red coat at the base of an oak tree. She keeps barking, looking down at a strange heap on the forest floor.

I don't understand what I'm looking at until I notice the heap is wearing a navy-blue work shirt.

*Grandpa. Oh, God, it's Grandpa.*

I start running, and for several seconds, all I hear is my pounding heart.

I kneel by his side, put my hand on his shoulder, and gently shake him. "Wake up, Grandpa."

He doesn't move. A couple leaves cling to his hair and his hat lies upside down a few feet away.

My stomach flutters, heartbeat racing faster, faster, as I look directly above, noticing the deer stand tied to the tree about twenty feet off the ground. My gaze skims over the stand's platform and ladder, and then falls back to Grandpa.

Realization makes my chest tighten and my mouth go dry. *Grandpa fell. Oh, God, Grandpa fell.*

I shake him again. "Grandpa, can you hear me?"

His eyes flutter open, and he looks up at me, blinking several times. "Clint, I need you to…need to go…" His eyes close and he winces.

"It's okay, Grandpa. You don't have to talk. Do you think you can stand?"

"No," Grandpa rasps, kind of like how he sounds in the morning before he's had his coffee. "I need you to…"

I look around until I spot Rhett, standing behind me with wide eyes. "Go back to the house and call 911. Quick!"

He doesn't even nod; he just turns on his heel and starts running back the way we came.

Sandy's stopped barking now, but she stares down at Grandpa and whines, like she knows something's wrong. "It's okay. Everything will be okay," I say to her, to Grandpa, to myself. Tears sting my eyes. *God, please let him be okay.*

Grandma clutches the steering wheel, her knuckles white, as she follows behind the ambulance to the hospital. Since we've gotten in the truck, I doubt we've said ten words to one another. Any other time, I'd be too scared with Grandma behind the wheel, but now I'm too upset and worried.

*God, please don't take Grandpa from us,* I pray. *I don't want him to go. I don't want him to—*

Grandma slams on the brakes as the overhead traffic light turns red. "Dang it!" she yells, punching the steering wheel. "I don't have time for this!"

Rhett tenses beside me. "Grandma, don't yell—"

"Hush!" she screams.

Then she floors it, tires squealing, engine revving as she runs the red light and chases after the ambulance.

I close my eyes and pray harder.

We stay in the hospital waiting room for what feels like days, even though it's probably only been an hour. When your only company is a hyperactive seven-year-old and a sixty-eight-year-old on the verge of a nervous breakdown, an hour can feel like forever.

All of a sudden, Grandma stands from her chair and goes over to the front desk.

"Can you find out if I can go back there now?" she asks the woman behind the desk. If I had to guess, she's asked that question ten times since we got here.

"They're still working on him, ma'am," the woman says.

Grandma sighs and walks back to her seat.

My chest feels like a tangle of Christmas lights. *If only I'd helped him put up the deer stand,* I think, my stomach rolling like it does when I'm sick. *Then he would be okay. Then he wouldn't have fallen.* "Do you think he's going to be alright?" I ask Grandma.

She doesn't answer me. She just stares down at the floor, tapping her foot.

She looks a mess—perspiration gleams on her forehead, sweat stains her shirt under her arms, and her curly gray hair sticks up in several different directions from where she ran her fingers through it a couple minutes ago.

I ask her again, "Do you think he's going to be alright?"

She looks at me, her bottom lip trembling. "I don't know," she whispers.

Before I can ask anything else, she gets up and goes back over to the front desk.

"I'm bored," Rhett says once she's gone. "What do you think we should do?"

I point to the small TV hanging in a far corner of the room. "We can watch cartoons."

"But there's no sound. How about a board game?"

I stare at him for a moment. "What do you mean? Hospitals don't have board games."

"Yes, they do! Look," he says, pointing across the room to a small table. "Someone left their game. Looks like they didn't even finish playing."

"I don't know, Rhett," I say, shaking my head. "That probably belongs to someone else."

Just as soon as the words leave my mouth, Rhett's sitting at the table, picking up a silver game piece.

"Rhett," I groan, hurrying over. "Did you hear me?"

"What?" he says, holding up his hands. "Why can't we play?"

"Because," I say, "it's not ours."

At that moment, a woman walks through the waiting room doors several feet away from our table. She glances over at us and smiles. "You boys are more than welcome to play with that," she says, motioning to the board game. "Another family left it a couple nights ago."

When she turns away, Rhett smiles at me. "See? What did I tell you? Now sit down so we can start."

I pull out a chair from the table. "Whatever."

"It's my favorite game," Rhett says.

"What?"

Then I notice the stack of colored money in Rhett's hand.

"Monopoly?" I groan. "But I *hate* monopoly."

Rhett frowns. "Why? It's so fun!"

"Your definition of fun is different than mine. Monopoly takes forever."

Rhett shrugs. "It's not like we've got anything else to do."

I look around the small waiting room. A couple sits beneath the TV, staring down at their phones. Another man has his head leaned back and his eyes closed, mouth hanging slightly open. Grandma paces the floor near the front desk, her lips moving like she's mumbling to herself.

I turn back to Rhett. "Okay," I tell him. "But I get to roll first."

# 23

## BAD NEWS

BY THE TIME the doctor finally comes to see Grandma, Rhett and I have played three rounds of Monopoly. We set down our dice and money long enough to listen to their conversation.

"We have him stable, and we think we've stopped the internal bleeding," the man in green scrubs says to Grandma. "We're about to move him to Intensive Care."

"Intensive Care? What do you mean *Intensive Care*? What's wrong with him?" says Grandma.

The doctor's face grows serious, and he puts a hand on her shoulder. "Mrs. Boone," he says, bending down to her height, "I'm afraid I have some bad news. Your husband has a ruptured spleen, a punctured lung, two broken ribs, a compound fracture in his left leg, and internal bruising."

Grandma doesn't speak for a moment. "Oh gosh," she finally whispers. "What does this mean?"

"The next twenty-four hours are the most critical. They will determine if he is going to recover or not."

"You mean, he could *die*?" The word makes my stomach churn.

"Yes, ma'am. I'm afraid so."

Grandma looks away, shaking her head back and forth. "I told him not to fool around with that deer stand. I shouldn't have let him put it up in the first place. It's too dangerous."

"We won't know if he needs additional surgery until we finish running our tests and X-rays," the doctor says. "In the meantime, if you need anything, please let one of us know."

"I just need my husband to come home. That's all," Grandma says. "We've got two boys to raise."

I look down at our game, but I no longer want to play.

For dinner, we eat Doritos and Oreos from the vending machine down the hall, and when it's close to our bedtime, we gather in the ICU waiting room, where Grandma says we'll be staying the night. A kind nurse gives each of us a blanket to make our stay a little more comfortable. Still, I'm not sure I'll be able to sleep.

For a long while, we all watch *America's Got Talent* on a TV mounted to a far wall.

"Look, it's the ventriloquist," I tell Grandma, pointing at the screen, hoping it will brighten her spirits. "She's the one you like so much."

"That's crazy," Grandma says with a small grin, but I can tell it's forced. She has a glassy look in her eyes tonight, like she's staring through the TV, not really watching it.

"What's a ventriloquist?" Rhett asks in the chair beside me.

"A person who can talk without moving their lips. They use a puppet to make it look like the puppet can talk."

"Hey, I can do that!" Rhett makes a hand puppet. As he talks, he moves his fingers. "My name is Clint and I have a crush on Aaliyah and my brother is really cool and smart—"

"Stop it," I groan. "You're such a loser."

Grandma stands and walks out of the waiting room. It's the third time she's done that tonight.

"Hey, where's she going?" Rhett asks, staring after her.

He's asked that three times now, and every time, I tell him the same thing. "She's going to see Grandpa. He can only have short visits at a time. We're not allowed to see him since we're kids."

"What? That's not fair!"

"None of this is fair," I say, blowing out a sigh. My heart thuds in my chest, my arms and legs heavy, like how they get after I've spent an entire day working with Grandpa on the farm—driving fence posts, carrying long, thick branches to the burn pile, and raking fresh-cut grass to feed the cows. Only, this time, the heaviness isn't from physical labor. Instead, it's guilt for failing to keep Grandpa safe.

I close my eyes and picture Grandpa in the deer stand, shifting on his foot too fast, stepping wrong, and toppling over the side of the platform, his body thudding against the ground twenty feet below. My stomach roils again as the moment replays over and over in my mind. *If only I'd been there. If only I'd helped him.*

When I finally open my eyes, I notice Rhett curled up in his chair, asleep.

While I wait for Grandma to return, I look up at the ceiling and take a deep breath, thinking about Grandpa. I think of him shoving his feet inside his muddy boots just after breakfast, mumbling, "I've got work to do." I think of him watching the same western for the hundredth time. I think of him starting up conversations with strangers in Piggly Wiggly, restaurants, and even those strangers broken down on the side of the road, like that Hispanic couple who couldn't speak a lick of English. I think about when he laughs so hard that he has to grasp the dining room table to keep from falling over, cheeks just as red as when he comes inside after a long day of work. I think of his talk on the porch with me about Vietnam and survival. I think of him whistling Hank Williams' "Hey, Good Lookin'."

Then comes the memory that makes my throat burn: the day I first saw Grandpa cry.

That day, the sky was dark gray, and rain struck the metal roof as the wind whistled a lonesome tune. "Go check on your grandpa," Grandma told me, thumbing through a *Southern Living* magazine. "He'd appreciate the company."

"Why's that?" I asked, sitting up on the couch. "Is something wrong with him?"

"He gets sad sometimes, like we all do. Go upstairs and see him. You don't have to say anything. Just being there is enough."

I didn't argue; honestly, I was thankful for an excuse to do something other than watch the rain fall in sheets while Grandma commented on every recipe in *Southern Living*.

"*Corn pudding casserole...well, I declare.*"

"*Salted caramel apple sheet cake...well, butter my backside and call me a biscuit.*"

"*Purple sweet potato pie...reckon I'll pass on that one.*"

I found Grandpa upstairs, lying on my bed with his hands propped atop his chest. His eyes were closed, and for a moment, I thought he might be asleep.

"Grandpa?"

His eyes remained closed.

"Grandpa?" I said again, louder this time. His eyes opened. "Grandpa, I'm here."

He sat up and looked at me. "Hey, feller. Watcha know good?"

"Not much," I said. "What're you doing up here?"

"Just resting. Needed to get away from Ella and that mouth of hers. It's finally quiet."

I smiled, but I didn't believe him. "Are you okay?"

Grandpa sighed. Outside, thunder rumbled. "No, Clint. I reckon I'm not."

"What's wrong?"

"Well, it's hard to explain."

I sat beside him on the bed. "You can tell me."

Grandpa stared down at his hands. I noticed his nails were bitten to the quick, the skin around them bloody and raw, just like mine.

"I don't know if it would make sense."

"I'm sure it would."

There was a long pause. Then, in a soft voice, Grandpa said, "Do you remember when we were at the store the other day and that lady asked everyone for help except...well, except for me?"

"I do."

"Do you remember when we waited and waited in the doctor's office last week because they skipped my name, forgot about me entirely?"

"I do. And when you reminded the woman at the front desk about your appointment, she just looked at you funny and rolled her eyes."

"That's right. And do you remember when that waitress at that burger joint never came over to take our order?"

"I do. And then Grandma got upset and we had to leave. It made me sad."

We fell silent, the only sound the tapping of the rain against the roof.

Finally, Grandpa said, "People don't see you when you're older. People like me and Ella...it's like we're invisible. That's how I feel...invisible."

I looked at him for a moment, looked at the wrinkles on his face, the creases under his eyes, the faint white stubble along his jaw, the ruddiness of his nose, his cheeks. I loved his wrinkles, loved the lines of wisdom on his brow, his forehead. Loved his calloused hands, the healthy red of his skin, the hairs on his head resembling pale-gray toothbrush bristles. "I can't imagine not seeing you, Grandpa." A tear slid down his cheek, catching in the corner of his mouth. "You'll never be invisible to me."

Thinking of that day, and all the other little things about Grandpa that I love, makes my throat feel tight, so tight it's hard to breathe.

I recall what Grandpa said that morning on the porch, several days before I started sixth grade: *Getting older ain't all it's cracked up to be.*

Now, sitting in the ICU waiting room while Grandpa clings to life in a hospital bed somewhere close by, I understand what he meant: Getting older is realizing that who you love most will one day be gone.

## 24
## WORLD'S WORST WORRIER

I DON'T GET much sleep that night. Neither does Grandma. One time I woke up to hear her crying, which made me cry too. She wrapped her arms around me and kissed my forehead, told me everything would be alright.

I didn't believe her. Too many things had gone wrong in my life for something to finally go right. If my parents could die, Grandpa could too.

I wanted to ask her if he was any better, if he was coherent, but I couldn't do it. I didn't want her to lie to me, say *he's doing okay*. I heard what the doctor said: Grandpa has a ruptured spleen, a punctured lung, two broken ribs, and other serious injuries. I *know* he's not okay.

Early the next morning, Aunt Theresa picks me and Rhett up from the hospital and takes us to get breakfast before school. Even though I plead and beg Grandma to let us stay with her, she says we can't miss school, and that the hospital is no place for two boys to be hanging out.

"What about our backpacks? We can't go to school without our backpacks," I said to Grandma several minutes before Aunt Theresa showed up.

"Your aunt will swing you by the house to get your backpacks and some clean clothes. I'll give you my key."

"What about after school? We can't ride the bus home if no one is going to be there."

"Your aunt will take care of that. Just listen for her Cadillac in the pick-up line."

"What about—"

"Clint, drop it," Grandma said, pinching the bridge of her nose. "You're giving me a headache."

For breakfast, Aunt Theresa takes us to a restaurant called Wanda's Waffles. It's not that busy at six o'clock in the morning. Besides my aunt's white Cadillac, there are only four vehicles parked in the small lot.

Inside, the restaurant smells like bacon and maple syrup. Booths line two walls and several tables large enough to seat four people occupy the main floor. Nearly everything is red or white—the tables, the chairs, the booths, the walls, and the carpet. It honestly looks like a candy cane exploded in here. It's too bright, too cheerful-looking for a morning like this.

Once we're seated at a corner booth, a young, red-haired woman with split braids, a wide grin, and a white apron hurries over. "Howdy y'all," she says, placing one hand on her hip. "Welcome to Wanda's Waffles! What can I get the three of you started with this morning?"

I should probably return her smile, but to be honest, a smile's just not what I'm feeling.

After she writes down our orders on a little notepad—a pecan waffle for me, a Plain Jane waffle for Aunt Theresa, and a chocolate chip waffle for Rhett—our waitress retreats through the swinging door into the kitchen, practically bouncing the entire way there. I figure she's already had her morning cup of coffee, maybe two.

Next to me, Rhett props his elbows on the table and grins. "Want to hear a joke?"

"Sure," Aunt Theresa says, though it comes out sounding more like *shore*. "Ain't never turned down a good joke."

Rhett smiles wider. "Why do ducks have feathers?"

Aunt Theresa, while rubbing her thumb and forefinger against the checkered tablecloth, shrugs and says, "I reckon so they can fly."

"Nope. It's to cover their butt quacks!"

I roll my eyes while Aunt Theresa tosses her head back and cackles. To me, she sort of looks like a baby bird opening its mouth to be fed.

"I've got another one. Why did the bullet end up losing his job?" says Rhett.

"Why?" says Aunt Theresa.

"'Cause he got fired."

Aunt Theresa beats her fist against the table and cackles louder. If we weren't the only ones here, I'd be even more embarrassed than I already am.

Thankfully, our waitress comes back with our drinks, making Rhett and Aunt Theresa quiet down. Well, at least for a moment.

As she sets my glass of orange juice in front of me, Rhett asks the waitress, "Do you know any jokes?"

"Jokes?" The waitress puts a hand on her hip again. "Why I sure do! Wanna hear one?"

Rhett nods his head and flashes his tiny white teeth at her.

She says, "How do you kill a rodeo clown?"

"How?" Aunt Theresa and Rhett ask at the same time.

With a smirk, the woman says, "Go for the juggler!"

Rhett's beady eyes pinch together as he leans back, laughing so hard his caramel-colored cheeks turn bright red. His laughter makes my head hurt.

"My goodness," Aunt Theresa laughs, wiping tears. "That is *too* funny. My side's a hurtin'. Good one."

"My pleasure," the waitress says, smiling at us before bouncing away to the kitchen.

"I've got one," says Aunt Theresa. I notice she's no longer rubbing the tablecloth. Now she's got her pillowcase in hand, trailing her fingers down the fabric in scissoring motions. "It's a blonde joke. You like blonde jokes, Rhett?"

"You bet!" says Rhett.

"A blonde heard that most wrecks happen within four miles of a person's house. So you know what she did?"

"What?"

"She moved."

"I don't get it," Rhett says. Then Aunt Theresa glances at me and winks as she laughs at her own joke. "Clint, it's your turn. Know any jokes?"

"Uhhh, well...not really," I say, looking down at my lap.

"C'mon! I know you've got something to share with us," Aunt Theresa says.

"Okay. Well, I do know this one. Which US state is the most down to earth?"

They both stare at me.

"Floor-ida," I tell them.

They blink.

"Not funny," Rhett says, shaking his head. "I don't even get it."

"Hey, he tried, and that's all that matters," Aunt Theresa adds. "Ain't that right, Clint?"

"Yeah. Reckon so," I mumble, cheeks burning.

"Hey, Clint." Rhett nudges my shoulder. "Let me out for a sec. I've got to go use the bathroom."

"Okay."

Once Rhett's gone, Aunt Theresa looks at me and winks. "Don't let him give you a hard time." Lowering her voice, she says, "Are you alright? I know your grandpa gave us all a good scare."

"Not really," I tell her, my throat tightening. "I'm worried about him. If he doesn't get better, what's that mean for me, Rhett, and Grandma? She'll have to raise us by herself! What if it's too much and she decides she can't keep Rhett anymore? And what if—"

"Clint, that's enough." Aunt Theresa reaches for my hand across the table and squeezes it. "You've got to quit worryin'. It ain't good for ya. Take it from me: I used to be the world's worst worrier. 'Specially when Henry went off to fight in 'Nam. Heck, that's when I started twiddlin' like crazy. Mama told me worryin' is like sitting in a rockin' chair. It don't get you no further down the road." Aunt Theresa lets go of my hand and goes back to twiddling with her pillowcase. "Your grandpa is the strongest man I know. He'll get better. It might take a month of Sundays, but he'll pull through. 'Sides, he probably hurt himself worse jumpin' out of planes in 'Nam. Or that time Daddy ran him over with the tractor."

My eyes widen. "Grandpa was run over by a tractor?"

"That's beside the point," says Aunt Theresa. "The truth is: us old folk are tough, but we won't live forever."

"I wish Grandma and Grandpa could live forever. What am I supposed to do without them?"

Aunt Theresa shakes her head, locks of gray hair swaying around her face. "Ya better enjoy 'em while you've got 'em. Soak up every moment. Listen to every word. Tell 'em how much you love 'em. Things like that matter."

I nod. "I can do that."

Aunt Theresa smiles. "I think of my grandparents every day. There was nothin' they loved more than to talk, laugh, and tell stories, 'specially while they were shellin' peas. You wouldn't believe how many stories two people could tell. And I would always listen. Turns out you can learn a lot that way. And while they may not be around anymore, at least I have the memories."

"Grandma says memories keep a person alive long after they're gone."

"That's right," she says.

*But I don't want Grandpa to be just a memory*, I

think. *I want him* here. *I want him to be well again. Is that too much to ask?*

And the question I dread the answer to most of all: "What happens if Grandpa doesn't get better?"

Before she can say anything, Rhett is back, climbing over my lap to sit beside me.

Soon, the conversation shifts to more jokes, and I'm thankful. After all, there isn't anything Aunt Theresa could say to make me quit worrying.

# 25

## GRANDPA'S PROMISE

Paying attention in class is more difficult than ever. Not that it matters. No one pays me much mind, just like any other day. The teachers barely look in my direction, and my classmates don't speak to me. You'd think by now a teacher would've called me out for being unfocused, but I'm practically like an extra in the background of a movie—nearly invisible.

I have no one to talk to about Grandpa, no one except Aaliyah, who I won't see today since I'm not riding the bus. I can't stop thinking about him, wishing I was at the hospital instead of school. At least at the hospital you can watch TV to occupy your mind.

It's kind of crazy, but ever since Rhett fought Bart, and even with our conversation in the hall yesterday, Bart won't look at me. At least, not for long. If I do happen to catch him staring, he looks away before he can make it obvious. I thought that after Rhett kicked him on the school bus that Bart would find a way to get back at me. Maybe not in front of Rhett, and not in front of the students on the bus, but somewhere more private, like the restroom or even the janitor's closet. So, it's strange that he's stopped bothering me completely and that he just wants to be left alone.

Either way, without Bart pestering me, I should feel free, but I don't; somehow, I only feel more lonesome.

At lunch, I sit at the far edge of one of the dining tables, several seats away from everyone else. I unzip my backpack, pull out a book—*Alabama Moon* by Watt Key—and flip to the chapter I left off on the day before.

It takes me nearly the entire lunch period to get through a single page, and even when I do, I can't tell you anything I read. I can't remember, I can't concentrate, and I couldn't care less. It's hard to care about anything knowing that Grandpa might not recover and that Grandma is at the hospital all by herself. Just like me, I bet she has no one to talk to. I bet she feels as lonesome as I do.

Thinking about them, about the people I love most in distress, makes my chest ache and my throat burn. Silently, I lower my head onto the lunch table and begin to cry.

If only I had that birthday card—the one that plays my parents' voices when I open it. The one where they tell me they love me. I could listen to their voices all day, and they wouldn't get old. Maybe they would calm me down. Comfort me. Not make me feel so empty and alone.

"Hey."

The soft voice comes from behind, but I don't respond. Maybe if I don't give any indication that I heard, whoever it is will just go away. Besides, they're probably not talking to me anyway.

The lunch table shakes a little as someone sits down beside me.

"Hello?"

My chest tightens as I recognize the voice, louder this time. Quickly wiping away my tears, I lift my head up from the lunch table and look at the person sitting beside me.

I blink once. Twice.

It's Bart, staring at me with his eyebrows raised.

I swallow, heart pounding. Surely he won't start anything in the middle of the cafeteria. That'll only draw a crowd, but maybe that's what he wants. Maybe he wants nothing more than to finally punish me for kicking him and for Rhett fighting him on the bus. Maybe he doesn't care if everyone watches. What does he have to lose?

The thought makes my heart race faster.

"Are you okay?" he asks, and my mouth drops open. *What did he just say?*

"Not really." I wipe my eyes again and take a deep breath. "What do you want?"

Bart doesn't seem to hear me. "What's the matter with you? What's got you so upset?"

"Nothing." If anyone deserves to know what happened to Grandpa, it's definitely not Bart. Why is he sitting next to me? He doesn't even *like* me.

"Well, it looked like you were upset."

"What do you care?" I blurt. "Everyone else around here acts like I'm invisible. Why can't you?"

He sighs. "Jesus, Cowgi—*Clint*. You're not the only one who feels that way. Invisible, I mean."

I blink. Bart feels invisible? Well, maybe if he wasn't so mean, people would want to hang around him. Maybe it's his own fault that no one pays him any mind.

"Why are you talking to me? I thought you hated me."

Bart snorts. "I don't hate you. I don't hate anyone. I'm just…"

"You're just *what*?"

"Sad. There, Clint, I said it. I'm just *sad*."

*So am I,* I think, but I bite the words back.

I was expecting Bart to admit that he's mad or even humiliated for what Rhett did to him. But *sad*? What for?

Before I can ask, the bell rings, and the noise in the cafeteria swells as students zip up their lunchboxes, throw away their plastic trays, and shove past one another, shoes squeaking on their way out the door.

"See you later," Bart mumbles, standing from the table. I watch him as he walks away, staring down at the floor, shoulders slumped, back hunched. He does look sad, which only makes me more confused.

Maybe Bart's going through more than I realize. Maybe I don't really know Bart at all.

It's strange how bad days seem to last forever while good days seem to never last long enough. At the hospital that afternoon, it seems like a whole week instead of a day has passed since Grandpa fell from the deer stand. Standing in the hall outside Grandpa's room, my sadness is reflected on Grandma's puffy face and swollen eyes, and I know she feels the same constant ache in her chest as I do.

"It's time," Grandma tells me. "The doctors woke him up so you can talk to him. But he's in a lot of pain; you won't be able to stay in there long."

"What else did the doctors say?"

She motions toward the door. "Go."

I do as she says.

Inside Grandpa's room, the air is cold and smells like floor cleaner. Monitors beep and click. A muted TV mounted to the wall plays a western. It almost makes me smile, but then I notice the bed in the center of the room…and the still form lying on top of it.

At the sight of him, I suck in a breath. It's like I'm at a museum, studying Grandpa through a glass case, like something too frail and fragile to be touched, only observed.

"Are you okay?"

It's a stupid question, really. With one look at all the yellow and purple bruises along his arms, and the tubes stuck into his veins and the wires taped to his skin, I can see he's not okay.

"Feelin' fine as wine," Grandpa mutters.

I smile, but I know he's lying. "I won't keep you long."

Grandpa takes a deep breath. "I'm glad you're here, Clint."

Every word from his mouth sounds strained and labored. He's never sounded this weak before, this exhausted. It scares me. I just want him to get well. Any day now, the hurt will go away and the doctors will let Grandpa go home, where he's supposed to be.

"Son," he says with a grimace, like the word physically hurts. He pats the spot beside him on the bed. Once I sit down, he continues. "Son, I don't believe I'll be here much longer."

"What do you mean? You look better. And you're talking! That's good, isn't it?"

His calloused hand grips my own, but it only feels cold. "I can always talk. Don't matter if I'm half dead," he says. Wincing, he takes another deep breath. "I just wanted to see you, in case…in case it's the last time." His pale blue eyes fill with tears. Then he lets go of my hand and looks at me. Really looks at me, his eyes staring into mine, unblinking. His fingers touch my face, carefully, as if I'm something that might break. "You mean the world to me," he whispers. "You always have."

My throat burns. "Grandpa, don't talk like that. You have to get better. You *have* to."

His hand falls from my face onto the white sheets, but he keeps looking at me. "I'm sorry, but I don't think I can fight it this time."

The burn in my throat intensifies. My vision blurs. "But I"—I take a breath, wipe my eyes— "I don't want you to go."

"Son," he says, so soft I barely hear him. "Life's like a vapor. We're not promised tomorrow."

"I know, and it's not fair."

"Nothing about life is fair. If it was, I wouldn't be in this hospital bed right now, or a place where I can't even get a decent glass of sweet tea." He takes my hand again. "I want you to make me a promise. Watch out for your grandma while I'm gone. Rhett, too. Don't let him get into any trouble."

"Yes sir," I tell him, sniffling. "I promise."

"And I hope you haven't forgotten what I always tell you."

"What's that?"

"That all this," he says, pointing a finger around the room, and then pointing it back at himself, "will change. That's just life. But there are two things I guarantee will always stay the same."

"Sweet tea and snap peas," I whisper.

He tries to smile, but it looks pained. "That's right."

I lean forward and slowly, carefully, put my arms around him. Just in case…in case it's the last time. I wonder: *Why do the best things always have to go?*

Tears spill down my cheeks now. "I love you, Grandpa."

He nods and closes his eyes for a moment. When he opens them, tears start spilling down his cheeks too. "You've given me my best years," he says.

For a while, we don't speak, the only sounds the beep and click of monitors. When I look toward the door and scoot to the edge of the bed, he says, "Your grandma will come get you when she's ready."

Something in the way he says it makes my throat tighten. I force down a shaky breath. "She said I wouldn't be able to stay long."

"You can stay as long as you want, Clint. As long as you want."

"But I don't want to upset you."

"You ain't done it."

"I made you cry."

"Ain't nothing wrong with that."

"I'm sorry."

"What for?"

"For making you sad."

With a weak smile, he says, "You make my heart too full to be sad."

I don't know what to say; I just fiddle with my hands, staring down at my chewed fingernails. We fall into silence again, but it isn't awkward or uncomfortable. Instead, it's peaceful—a silence that only exists with someone you love.

"I wish I had more time," Grandpa says finally, the words a whisper. "Seventy years sounds like forever when you're young, doesn't it? But it's not. It's just a blink. Really no time at all." He pauses. "But I can't think of any better way to spend the last of it than with you."

"How do we make it worth it then?" I ask.

He's silent for a moment, staring at something behind me. Then his gaze meets mine. "My whole life I've told you stories. Now I want you to tell me one."

"I don't know many stories."

"Sure you do."

"Well, I wouldn't be very good at it. It'd probably be something stupid."

"No story is stupid. Tell me one."

When I hesitate, he says, "Go ahead, Clint. Just try."

And so, before I even realize it, I start telling him about Aaliyah and Bart and even Rhett, like when he keeps me up at night talking. I also tell him about that day on the bus when Rhett stood up for me. It's something I've never told anyone else, something that was meant to stay a secret between me and Rhett. Even so, the words escape without much thought, like I've needed to get them out for a long time. Once I start talking, I can't stop. All the while, Grandpa stares at me, a calmness behind his eyes. He doesn't look like he's in pain anymore.

When I'm done telling my story, I say, "Well, how was it?"

He smiles. "It's the best thing I've ever heard."

# *26*
## THINGS YOU CAN'T SAY

THE NEXT DAY, I'm in third period when the intercom buzzes and something strange happens—I hear *my* name.

*Clint Boone to the main office please,* the speaker crackles. *Tell him to bring his things.*

Everyone in class looks around, probably wondering: *Who's Clint Boone?*

When I stand from my desk, I feel all of their eyes on me. No one speaks. No one utters a sound. Typically when someone is sent to the main office, they're in trouble. *Big* trouble. They probably think the same applies to me.

I hope that's the case. Deep down, I think I know the real reason why I won't be returning, and being in trouble sounds better than the alternative.

"Clint, are you alright?"

The voice comes from the front of the room. I turn to look—it's my teacher, Ms. Hare. It's the first time she's spoken to me all school year.

"No," I tell her, the word sounding hoarse because of my sore throat and lungs. "Not at all."

Then I open the door and step into the hall.

In the office, Aunt Theresa is sitting in one of the blue plastic chairs, waiting for me.

The moment I step through the doors and meet her red, swollen eyes, I know why she's here. Stuffing her pillowcase in her purse and slinging the strap over her shoulder, she hurries over to me and wraps me up in a big hug.

My knees feel weak, and I hold onto my aunt to keep myself upright. "He's gone, isn't he?" I mumble into her shoulder.

"Yeah, baby," she says, stroking my head. "I'm sorry."

After we pick Rhett up from the elementary school, Aunt Theresa says she wants to take us out for ice cream. I guess she thinks that will cheer me up, but ice cream is the last thing on my mind.

For a while, Rhett seems oblivious to our silence, until he notices the tears rolling down Aunt Theresa's cheeks. He looks up at me in the backseat, his eyes shiny. "Grandpa isn't coming home, is he?"

I shake my head. Rhett's bottom lip trembles.

"He loved you, buddy," I say, placing an arm over his shoulder and holding him close. "He loved you so much."

"Then why did he leave me? Why couldn't he *stay*?"

*Because life isn't fair,* I think.

In the end, I don't say anything. There are just some things you can't say to a seven-year-old.

Back at home, I shut myself inside my room, and open the drawer with my parents' birthday card. Right now, I need to hear their voices. I need to hear something comforting, something familiar.

I open the card, but there's no sound.

My mother's voice doesn't play like it always does. She doesn't tell me she loves me. My father doesn't cut in with his quip about cake either.

*Maybe it's just a mistake,* I think.

I close the card and open it again.

Still nothing.

I close it; open it; close it; open it—

"Mom! Dad!" I cry out. "Talk to me! I need you!"

Silence.

I throw the card down beside me and put my face in my hands.

I've lost them again.

I've lost Grandpa.

I've lost *everything*.

Tears spill from my eyes and down my cheeks. My

chest aches, my heart aches. My breath hitches, and I gulp down air, too much, too fast.

There's the creak of the bedroom door, then the patter of footsteps.

"Clint?"

I don't look up.

"*Clint?*" The voice sounds both sharp and broken, and I lift my face from my hands. Even through the blurriness in my wet eyes, I can make out Rhett's wrinkled white T-shirt, his baggy blue jeans, and ruffled black hair. His brown eyes glisten with tears.

I throw my arms around him, pulling him close until my face is buried in his shoulder. He whimpers as his body trembles and his warm tears drip down my neck. I hug him tighter. The way I should've hugged Mom and Dad before they got in that car wreck. The way you hug someone to keep them from leaving. To keep them safe.

I don't want to ever let go.

"I've got you," I tell him. "Thank God I've got you."

As Rhett wraps his arms around me too, squeezing tight, I realize that I haven't lost everything. Not even close.

## 27
## THE CALL

I DON'T GO to school for the rest of the week. Instead, I stay home with Rhett and Grandma. Rhett took it hard the day he found out Grandpa died, but it didn't take him long to revert back to his normal, hyperactive self.

When he and I aren't spending time in our fort at the edge of the woods, having Nerf gun battles, water fights with the garden hose, or walking along the creek, searching for arrowheads, we're watching movies with Grandma and listening to her stories.

Grandpa's death turns out to be the most difficult change for all of us. He's like the one missing piece that completes the whole puzzle. Without him, it's just not the same. The house is quieter now. Empty. Just like Grandpa's recliner and his seat at the dining room table. He might not be here in person anymore, but there are traces of him everywhere—in our house, on our farm, in my mind. Lately, I've been thinking about how those we love never really die because our memory keeps them alive.

I'm going to keep Grandpa alive forever.

I'm not the only one struggling with his absence, either. The other night, when I got up to get a glass of water from the kitchen sink, I noticed the light under Grandma's bedroom door. I stopped and listened long enough to hear her on the other side, weeping.

Lately, I've taken Aunt Theresa's words to heart and tell Grandma I love her as much as I can. You'd be surprised how much that helps. Life is too short not to tell someone you love them.

Ms. Jean brought us a pound cake when she heard the news. Myrtle brought us a peach cobbler, and Aunt Theresa brought us a big box of fried chicken, just so Grandma wouldn't have to cook for a while. I'll admit: it's been strange seeing Aunt Theresa step up this past week. Even stranger is watching Grandma let her.

If anything resulted from Grandpa's death, it's that Grandma and Aunt Theresa have grown closer. Isn't it odd how death brings people together? I wonder how Grandpa would feel knowing they're on amicable terms now.

Whenever Aunt Theresa's around, Grandma puts on a show, laughing and pretending that everything is normal. But the moment she's gone, that faraway look returns to Grandma's eyes and her gaze goes cold. It's impossible to know what she's thinking when she gets like that.

One afternoon, coming inside for a quick water break after leaving Rhett alone in our fort, I hear Grandma talking in her bedroom.

Creeping down the hall, I stop outside her door and listen.

"I'm sorry if I'm bothering you," she says, speaking softly. "I just have some concerns I'd like to share. Do you have a moment?"

I lean closer, placing my ear against the door to hear her better. She's talking on the phone. But to who?

Grandma sighs. I imagine her sitting on the edge of the bed, looking down at the floor. "What do we need to do if I decide I can't do this? Rhett's a good kid, but raising two boys on my own is too much. It's just too much."

My stomach clenches with the realization: *Grandma is giving Rhett up.*

*No,* I think. *Nononono. She can't do that.*

"Yes. I see. I understand. Let us get through the funeral first, and then we can talk about a date. I want to make sure we have enough time to say our goodbyes."

I take a deep breath. This is exactly what I was afraid of. If some person comes to take Rhett away, there's a good chance I'll never see him again.

At the thought, a hard lump forms in my throat.

Maybe this is why, deep down, I never wanted to grow close to Rhett in the first place. Maybe I knew all along that, one day, I would have to let him go, and I wouldn't be ready.

I don't think I'll ever be ready. Rhett can't go. He just can't. Losing him to a different family will be like a death.

Without another thought, I grab the doorknob and turn it, then step inside Grandma's room.

She's sitting on the bed, just as I suspected, the phone held to her ear.

She looks up at me. "Clint? Please give me a—"

"No," I tell her.

She lowers the phone onto her lap, placing one hand over the receiver. "What did you just say?"

"No," I tell her again. "Rhett is one of us. He's family. He has to stay."

Grandma stares at me for a moment. Then she raises the phone to her ear and says, real chipper, "Ms. Nance? I'll call you back. I've got to go." When she hangs up, she rises on her feet and takes a step toward me. Her lips are pursed, her eyes narrowed to slits. I've never seen her look so angry. "You have no business talking to me that way, you hear? You're just a child. You don't understand what this is like! It's a financial burden, and it's too much for a woman my age to put up with on her own. So don't come in here telling me what I can and cannot do—"

I block her before she can storm out of the room. Her mouth falls open. "Clint, what has gotten into you?"

I've never stood up to her before, and she knows it. Never. But this is different, this is *Rhett*. Rhett, who flooded Ms. Jean's yard, chased Josephine's glass eye down the church aisle, and kicked Bart straight between the legs. Rhett, who distracts me from my homework and gets on my nerves often.

My *brother*, Rhett.

I'm not about to let her give him away. And I'll stand up for him too, no matter what, because it's the least I can do for a kid who's never known what it's like to be appreciated.

"I lost my parents, I lost Grandpa, and I can't lose

Rhett too." Something hot and wet streaks down my cheeks. "He's like a snap pea, remember? He might be tiny, but someone's got to give him a fightin' chance."

Grandma looks down. Her voice is more tender than ever. "A snap pea. That's right...I said that, didn't I?"

I sniffle and wipe my nose with the back of my hand. "We won't cost you much. I promise. We can help out. I'll get a job, make some extra money for us. I can do it. I *can*. Just let him stay. Give him a chance, Grandma. Please, just give him a chance—"

"Okay! *Okay*." She takes a deep breath, puts a hand to her forehead. "You're right. I'm sorry. I haven't been thinking straight. Please...forgive me."

I step forward and wrap my arms around her.

Then, with her face pressed against my neck, she starts to cry.

"It's okay. You're okay," I tell her.

She sobs harder, her body quivering. "It's just too much...too much..."

"I know. But don't worry. I'll take good care of Rhett."

She makes a sniffling sound. "I know you will."

Still holding on to her, I say, "Even if he gets on my nerves, I promise I'll put up with him, 'cause he deserves a chance."

"He does. He sure does."

I hug her tighter. "And I love you, Grandma. You and Rhett both. No matter what happens. I can't imagine life without y'all."

# 28

## A BROTHER LIKE YOU

A FEW DAYS later, on a Saturday afternoon, we gather at Magnolia Springs Church for Grandpa's funeral. I'm sitting in one of the front pews, watching the slideshow of his life before the service starts, when someone taps me on the shoulder and whispers my name.

My blood turns to ice. The hairs on the back of my neck stand on end. I'd recognize that voice anywhere.

Slowly, I turn and look up.

"Bart?" I whisper back.

Bart stares down at me, but instead of looking angry or annoyed like usual, he just looks sad, sort of like in the cafeteria the other day.

"What are you doing here?" I ask him.

Beside me, Rhett tenses. He turns around in the pew and fixes Bart with a nasty look, his eyes narrowed, teeth bared like Sandy whenever she spots a squirrel darting around the yard.

"Uhhh…" Rocking back on his heels, Bart looks at Rhett cautiously before directing his gaze back to me, eyebrows raised. "He's not going to kick me again, is he?"

"No," I say. Then, to Rhett, I whisper, "Don't try anything."

I look back at Bart. He's wearing a crisp blue polo and khaki pants.

"I'm sorry about your grandpa," he says, stuffing his hands in his pockets.

"Thanks."

"He looked like a real nice man."

"He was." Bart keeps standing there, looking sad, until I pat the spot between me and Rhett and tell him, "C'mere. Have a seat."

Rhett frowns as Bart plops down in the middle of the pew. I bet he's just as confused as I am. Why is Bart here? Why is he being so nice all of a sudden?

Just before I can ask him, Bart says, "I didn't realize Henry was your grandpa. My dad worked with him at the mechanics shop a few years ago. Said your grandpa taught him everything he knew."

"Oh." *Bart's dad knew Grandpa? What a small world.*

"I'm really sorry, Clint"—Bart sighs—"for being such a jerk. I know how hard it is to lose someone you love because…"

Bart stops talking. Then the weirdest thing happens: he begins to cry.

I blink several times, unsure if what I'm seeing is real.

Is the same guy who broke my sandal and spit in my face actually *crying*?

Oh God. What am I supposed to do? Pat him on the back? Tell him it'll be alright?

I look at Rhett over Bart's shoulder, whose wide eyes let me know he's just as startled as I am. I'm about to go find Grandma—after all, she'll know what to do—when Rhett does something weird too: he starts patting Bart's back.

"It's okay," Rhett whispers. "You're okay."

Bart only sobs harder. "My m-mom…I lost my mom. She had c-cancer."

My heart sinks. "Bart—"

"After she died, I was angry at everything. I didn't know what to do without her. I still don't."

I fish out a tissue from my pocket and hand it to him.

"Thanks," he says, blowing his nose into it with the force of an elephant. "I promise I don't usually cry."

I'm pretty sure the entire church can hear us, but I don't look around long enough to see who's watching. Instead, I put my hand on Bart's shoulder and say, "It's okay to cry. Trust me, it really helps."

Bart sniffles. A tear drips from his chin as he turns to look at me, his eyes red and puffy. "I probably look like a big baby."

"No, you don't. You look just like the rest of us."

I hand Bart the pack of tissues from my pocket. After all, he needs it more than I do.

"I'm sorry, Clint," he says, wiping his nose with a tissue. "You don't have to forgive me. I was just going through a lot and I wanted to take it out on someone. Doesn't make it right."

"I understand."

He leans back against the pew and takes a deep breath. "You're right. Crying does help."

"Feel better now?"

He nods. "Better."

After the graveside service, while Grandma and Aunt Theresa hug and shake hands with everyone beneath the funeral home's red tent, I walk with Rhett through the cemetery.

"Now that Grandpa's gone, we've got to step up," I tell him. "That means more chores and more responsibility. Grandma can't keep the farm running all by herself. Understand?"

"Yeah," Rhett says, kicking at a piece of gravel with the pointed toe of his cowboy boot. "I just hate it."

"Hate what?"

"That Grandpa had to leave us. Why couldn't things stay like they were?"

"It's called change, Rhett. I don't like it either. But it's necessary. It's a part of life."

"Well, it's dumb," Rhett says, crossing his arms.

"Maybe," I say, "but if it weren't for change, you wouldn't be here."

"Yeah, I know. And I never would've met you or Grandpa or Grandma."

"That's right. See? Change isn't all that bad. Sometimes, it can be a good thing. It just takes a while to get used to."

"I probably took a while to get used to, didn't I?"

"Yeah. You sure did. But I'm glad you're here." I take a deep breath. "It took me a long time to accept my parents' deaths. But Grandma says something good that comes out of a bad situation is that God puts great people in your path, and I think God sent you to me to make me feel purpose in life again."

Rhett stops walking and looks up at me. The soft breeze ruffles his curly black hair. "I've always wanted a brother like you," he says.

Just like that, my throat starts to burn. I drag in a breath as my eyes water.

A moment later, while looking past me at the trees bordering the graveyard, Rhett says, "You think they have sweet tea and snap peas in heaven?"

"Of course I do."

"Then Grandpa should be okay."

"Don't worry. He'll be fine." I nudge Rhett's shoulder. "And so will we."

For a long while, we don't say another word. We just walk among the tombstones, listening to the gentle wind breathing through the treetops and the comforting song of the cicadas; meanwhile the golden sun hovers on the horizon among wispy clouds, most of them pink, others a dusty orange like brewed tea.

Then Rhett begins to whistle—softly at first, then louder, the melody becoming more recognizable.

It's "Hey, Good Lookin'" by Hank Williams.

We start walking toward the tent where Grandma

and Aunt Theresa are still hugging necks and Grandpa's shiny casket rests atop a metal rack. On the way there, Rhett whistles and I hum along while mourners dressed in black make their way back to their cars on canes and aluminum walkers, probably hurrying to make it home in time for the next rerun of *Gunsmoke*.

# EPILOGUE

On my way to the picnic table at the end of the porch, I pass Grandpa's boots. The other day, I slipped them on, just to see how they felt. I was surprised to find that, despite the grime clinging to the soles, the worn-out strings, and the heaviness of the leather, the boots were quite comfortable.

Sitting around the picnic table with giant metal bowls of peas resting on their laps, are Rhett, Grandma, and Aunt Theresa. They're laughing. *Really* laughing. I could hear them all the way from inside the house.

The sound makes me smile. After six months of sadness, I believe laughter is the most beautiful sound on earth.

"Where do you want me to put it?" I ask.

Grandma's gaze darts to the large watermelon in my hands. "Put it right here," she says, pushing over my bowl of peas to make room in the center of the table. "Theresa, Rhett…get all you want. There's plenty more where that came from."

I'll admit it's still a little strange to hear Grandma talk so syrupy to Theresa, given their history. It's also strange how Bart is my new best friend now. We sit together in seventh period and at lunch. Probably the strangest of all is that Rhett sits beside Bart on the bus, while I sit across the aisle with Aaliyah. We're like four peas in a pod.

Grandma runs a hand through her bowl of peas, bringing her unshelled ones to the top. "I had a nightmare last night," she says with a shiver.

Rhett looks up from his bowl. "Oh no. What about?"

"Well," Grandma says, "this time the police were after me. And no matter what I did, I just couldn't get away. There were too many of 'em."

I roll my eyes, chuckling to myself. "You're always paranoid about the police. Did you rob a bank or something when you were younger? Is that why you're always so scared they're going to find you?"

Grandma scrunches up her brow and points a finger at herself. "Me? Now, Clint," she says, "you know I could never get away with something like that."

"What about in your dream?" Aunt Theresa adds, while using one of the kitchen knives to cut into the watermelon. Tucked beneath her thigh, I notice her new pale-green pillowcase, the one Grandma gave her to make up for the one Sandy destroyed.

"Well, I guess it's possible," Grandma says. "I really can't remember."

"Maybe you ran a red light, Grandma," says Rhett.

"Yeah. Or a stop sign," I say. "Or maybe she ran over someone."

"Boys!" Grandma scoffs. "Would you quit? It was just once. Okay, maybe twice."

"I understand, Ella," says Aunt Theresa. "I dream about running from the law all the time."

I shake my head. "Y'all are weird."

Grandma stops shelling long enough to sip from her tea glass. "Theresa," she says, setting the glass down with a loud clink, "did I ever tell you 'bout the time Henry drove off from the gas pump and forgot to remove the nozzle?" He snatched that hose right out of the pump and drug it down Main Street for a good two miles. Every time someone would honk or wave, he'd just wave back, like they were saying hello."

Aunt Theresa laughs so hard she almost spits up her watermelon.

Grandma shakes her head. "You should'a seen it...he had five cop cars on his tail at one point. He didn't even know they were chasing him! What happened next was even worse..."

While I listen to Grandma's story, I realize something: one day, I'm going to miss this. One day, life will snatch away moments like this, nothing left but a memory. But for now, I sit back and I listen, drinking tea, shelling peas, and laughing so hard my ribs hurt.

And for once, I don't worry about what comes next.

## ACKNOWLEDGMENTS

A special thanks to Nathaniel Allen, whose casual mention of snap peas inspired this story. It immediately made me think of my grandparents shelling peas in their living room, bickering back and forth in between sips of sweet tea.

Thanks to my beta readers: Katie Adams, Hope Allen, Ethan Howard, Tara Manson, Kristen Nelson, and Holly Sproule. Your feedback was invaluable and encouraged me to put this story out in the world.

I'd also like to thank my editor, Josh Vogt, for helping me make this story stronger and more focused. And the people at Damonza, the masterminds behind my book cover and so many wonderful others.

I'm eternally grateful to my parents, for their constant support, encouragement, and patience. Thank you for not forcing me into any career or life decisions, and not discouraging me when I said I wanted to become an author. Most of all, thank you for letting me dream, even now.

Finally, to my grandparents, the people behind the story. Thank you for the sweet tea, snap peas, game nights, terrifying car rides, chaotic church services, breakfast feasts, TV commentary, *Gunsmoke* marathons, fresh watermelon, late night stories of times past, and the pounds of baked lemon pepper chicken, which I dream of at least once (okay, twice) a week.

I can't imagine life without y'all.

## ABOUT THE AUTHOR

**McCaid Paul** is a Southern writer raised in the pines of rural Florida. He is the author of *Dead River*, *The Forgotten Headline*, *Mooch & Marlow*, and others. His short works have been published in the *Blackwater Review* of Northwest Florida State College. When he's not daydreaming about new stories, you can find him taking long hikes in the woods, fishing for hours at a time on the Choctawhatchee or drinking too much coffee and sweet tea. To learn more, visit him online at mccaidpaulbooks.com or on Instagram, Facebook, and TikTok @mccaidpaul.

Printed in the USA
CPSIA information can be obtained
at www.ICGtesting.com
LVHW040022230424
778120LV00002B/13

9 781735 729992